THE
SPIRITUALITY
OF
COMMUNION

Gerard Rossé

THE
SPIRITUALITY
OF
COMMUNION

A New Approach to the Johannine Writings

New City Press
Hyde Park, New York

Published in the United States by New City Press
202 Cardinal Rd., Hyde Park, NY 12538
©1998 New City Press

Translated by Matthew J. O'Connell from the original Italian
La spiritualità di comunione negli scritti giovannei
© 1996 Città Nuova, Rome, Italy

Cover design by Nick Cianfarani
Cover art: Ave Center, Loppiano, Italy

Library of Congress Cataloging-in-Publication Data:
Rossé, Gérard.
    [Spiritualitá di comunione negli scritti giovannei.   English]
    The spirituality of communion : a new approach to the Johannine
    writings / Gérard Rossé.
        p. cm.
    Includes bibliographical references.
    ISBN 1-56548-116-X
    1. Bible. N.T. John--Theology. 2. Bible. N.T. Epistles of
John--Theology.   3. Spiritual life--Christianity--Biblical teaching.
4. Community--Religious aspects--Christianity--Biblical teaching.
Title.
    BS2601.R67   1998
    226.5'06--dc21   98-11731

Contents

Preface

Theologian S. De Fiores recently gave expression to a need that is being strongly felt once again by Christians of our age—the need to live their faith in the company of others: "Persons are not pure interiority nor pure individuality, but are beings-in-relation, to the point that they cannot achieve their fulfillment apart from a community. This means the discrediting of a spirituality that is abstract, focused on the self, and individualistic, and that avoids the tasks of human beings in history."[1]

A few years earlier, in 1992, well-known ecclesiologist J. M. R. Tillard published a study with a significant subtitle: "The Sources of the Ecclesiology of Communion."[2]

Tillard wrote: "We may say . . . that for the common tradition of the early centuries, Christian life in all its aspects and all its parts is wholly a life as Church."[3] The author asks whether this ecclesial communion that is sealed

---

1. S. De Fiores, La "Nuova" Spiritualità (Rome: Ed. Studium, 1995) 19.
2. J. M. R. Tillard, Chair de l'Eglise, chair du Christ (Cogitatio Fidei 168; Paris: Cerf, 1992).
3. Ibid., 7.

by the eucharist and is constitutive of the being of a Christian has always been understood in the West. Did not the western Church, as judged by the mystics, favor "a communion with God by an individual alone with the Alone"? Tillard raises a question to which the answer is already clear: "Is the Church by any chance a communion of brothers and sisters, the purpose of which is that, fortified by the sacraments, they will help one another gain access to the experience of being alone with the Alone?"[4] In short, is the life of the Church meant only to promote the individual relationship of the soul with God?

But is this vision not precisely that of the so-called "Johannine mysticism" of the fourth gospel? True enough, the gospel of John has at times been accused of fostering a "soteriological individualism."[5] The impression that we may at first glance take from this gospel is indeed of a tendency to a spirituality focused on the self; the impression is caused by the dominant motif of faith that is seen as a profound personal encounter of the human being with Christ and by the typically Johannine use of the verb "contemplate." All this would seem to refer to an individualistic spirituality and be an invitation to a contemplative life that is isolated from the rest of humanity. R. Schnackenburg knows of that impression, but he responds to it without ambiguity: "This is, however, a deceptive impression, since the community of faith formed by Jesus himself is never entirely absent. Johannine Christianity is no different from the rest of early Christianity, in that it was

---

4. Ibid., 8.

5. See, e.g., C. F. D. Moule, "The Individualism of the Fourth Gospel," *Novum Testamentum* 5 (1962) 171-90.

convinced that Christian existence could not be realized outside or without the community."[6]

The aim of this book is to show, by means of a synchronic reading of the Johannine corpus, that the evangelist calls upon us to live our relationship with God, our life of faith, in and together with the community of believers, thereby championing a "spirituality of communion."

Gerard Rossé

---

6. R. Schnackenburg, *The Gospel according to John* 3, trans. D. Smith and G. A. Kon (New York: Crossroad, 1982) 209.

Chapter 1

Jesus: Revealer
and Revelation of God

1. Jesus, Exegete of God

The Prologue of the fourth gospel ends with a text that is a key to Johannine theology:

> No one has ever seen God:
> an only-begotten God (Son)[1] who is (turned)
> toward the bosom of God,
> he has told of him. (Jn 1:18)[2]

---

1. There is a textual problem in this verse. Some important manuscripts read: "*an* only-begotten God who is (turned) toward the Father" (or "*the* only-begotten God"); in fact, only God can reveal God. The idea is certainly Johannine, but the word *theos* (for the Son) would seem awkward after the initial *ton theon* (= the Father); but this variant is the *lectio difficilior* and to be preferred.

   Other manuscripts have: "the only-begotten Son," or "an only-begotten Son of God," or simply "the Only-Begotten."

2. How is the preposition *eis* (= toward) to be interpreted? In Koine Greek *eis* and *en* are often equivalent, and therefore the words may be translated: "who is in the bosom of the Father," thus bringing out the intimate communion of the Son with the Father.

   I. de la Potterie, *Gesù Verità* (Turin: Marietti, 1973) 192ff., maintains the pregnant sense of the preposition, that is, *eis* + accusative signifies a

The evangelist is stating, first of all, the absolute transcendence of God, in line with the great biblical tradition that is expressed, for example, in Exodus 33:20: "No human being can see me and remain alive."[3]

John does not mean to deny the possibility of a natural knowledge of God (see Wis 13; Acts 17:27f.; Rom 1:19f.). Rather, his interest is entirely concentrated on the second part of the verse: the fact that the revelation brought by Jesus, the incarnate Son, makes possible an authentic and definitive knowledge of God.[4]

The Son lives from eternity in the company of the Father, "turned toward" the bosom of the Father, which is the translation certainly to be preferred. "The constant directedness of the only-begotten Son toward the bosom of the Father as toward his origin . . . as toward the very source of his own life (*eis ton kolpon* = 'toward the bosom'), shows him in the eternal act of receiving the divine life from the Father."[5]

The choice of the expression "toward the bosom" sug-

---

movement or direction; he therefore translates: "The Son, turned toward the bosom of the Father . . . " The expression, he says, points to "that vital action with which the Word eternally moves toward the Father" (189, note 5). The inclusion with v. 1 should be noted.

The verb "to be" is in the form of the present participle, signifying a reality that abides: therefore the Son is permanently turned toward the Father and not simply before the incarnation or after his ascent to the Father as the glorified Lord.

The verb *exêgeisthai* normally has the meaning of "recount, describe, explain" (the noun "exegesis" is derived from it). Here, in an apocalyptic context, it can also have the meaning of "reveal divine secrets."

3. This motif is repeated in the Johannine writings: Jn 5:37; 6:46; 1 Jn 4:12, 20. It occurs frequently in the wisdom tradition (Sir 18:4; 43:31; Prv 30:4; etc.).

4. See the parallel text in John 6:46; see 3:13.

5. de la Potterie, *Gesù Verità*, 128.

gests an intimate relationship that unites Jesus, the Son, inseparably to the Father, and, following the line of the Old Testament, it also implies the idea of tender love.[6] " 'To be turned toward the bosom of the Father' marks the thrust of the Son's love toward the heart of the Father; it is his way of being *ab aeterno*."[7]

John's statement does not stop with this affirmation about the divine intimacy. The direct experience which the eternal Logos has of God is now manifested as a "word" that becomes "visible" in the words of Jesus.[8] The testimony of Jesus is truthful because it is based on his being that is turned permanently toward the bosom of the Father. He can make God known because he is God.

Precisely because Jesus is from eternity turned toward the Father, his revelation had an existential character that does not primarily consist in the teaching of a doctrine about God, but rather in letting the Father shine through him here on earth. The meaning of Jesus' message in the gospel of John is to be found in his own behavior. Jesus shows himself as "exegete" of the Father to the extent that he interprets his own existence and his own relationship to the Father as he lives it out in everyday life. He says this in a loud voice at the end of his public life: "Whoever sees me sees him who sent me" (Jn 12:45).

Jesus, therefore—the concrete Jesus in his behavior and his

---

6. "Toward the bosom" describes the loving attitude of spouses toward each other (Dt 13:7; 28:54, 56) or of a mother toward her child (1 Kgs 3:20; Ru 4:16; Is 49:22); see X. León-Dufour, *Lettura del Vangelo secondo Giovanni* (3 vols.; Cinisello-Balsamo, Milan: Ed. Paoline, 1989, 1992, 1995) I, 197.

7. Ibid.

8. León-Dufour, ibid., I, 200, notes that the verb *exêgeisthai* signifies an eye-witness's report of an event.

life as the Son—is the revelation of God to the extent that he reveals himself. Since Jesus is the Word permanently turned toward the Father, to know Jesus is to discover the relationship existing between the Son and the Father; it is to discover God as a communion of persons. "The relationship between Jesus the Son and the Father gives us an idea not only of the origin of Jesus and of the authority of his teaching, but it is also the essential content of the revelation of Jesus. In his teaching and in his very life he reveals nothing else but the Father; he is the revelation of the Father."[9]

These considerations show us the basic line of thought followed in John's gospel: Jesus speaks and acts as revealer by opening up to us the mystery of a person and a relationship. This is also the path on which the evangelist leads his readers. Fundamental to the fourth gospel is the call to see in the behavior of Jesus and in his message the origin of his very person, which is defined by his relation to the Father.

"The specific object of the revelation given by the man Jesus is the mystery of his person, the fact that he, the Son of God, is living in a unique relationship to the Father and that he invites us to share in his life as Son."[10]

2. Recognizing the Divine Origin of Jesus

In order to carry out his role as revealer of God in a convincing manner, Jesus needed first of all to have his divine origin recognized and accepted. This is the reason

---

9. L. Cilia, *La morte di Gesù e l'unità degli uomini (Gv 11, 47-53; 12, 32)* (Supplemento alla *Rivista Biblica*, 22; Bologna: EDB, 1992) 116.
10. de la Potterie, *Gesù Verità* (note 2, above) 196.

for the importance which the evangelist gives to the question of Jesus' origin: "Where does this man come from?"[11]

From this point of view, John 17:8 is a good summation of the mission of Jesus: "These have truly (re)cognized that I came from you, and they have believed that you sent me." The realization that Jesus came from the Father, that he is the one sent by the Father, contains the answer to the question of his origin. Recognition of the divine origin of Jesus means grasping the bond that unites him to the Father and defines him as Son. It is not enough for the Johannine Jesus to proclaim his own divinity, as if the mystery of his person meant that the man Jesus was a divinity in disguise and on a visit to humanity (the kind of thing that occurs in some stories in ancient mythology; for example, the episode of Philemon and Baucis). The divine identity of Jesus discloses a life of communion, a relationship that makes him the Son. It is this relationship, this close union with God, that the evangelist wants readers to discover on the basis of their own experience as disciples.

> What struck the beloved disciple was the fact that Jesus constantly spoke of the Father, saying that he was sent by the Father, that he came from close to the Father, that he always did the will of the Father and said only what he heard from the Father, that he was always in the Father and was returning to the Father. . . . He had gradually discovered in the man Jesus the life of the Son of God and that which was its secret: his relationship to the Father.[12]

---

11. Jn 7:27f.; 8:14; 9:29f.; 13:36; 19:9.
12. de la Potterie, *Gesù Verità*, 193.

The recognition of the divine origin of Jesus takes place at various levels: through the miracles, which John calls "signs" and which allow the glory of Jesus to shine through and are therefore a revelation of his person[13]; or through the revelatory discourses, which frequently interpret the miracles and in which Jesus makes known his role as Savior by means of some characteristic formulas that begin with "I am." But there is also a less visible level at which revelation no longer emerges from a miracle or a discourse but from the everyday behavior of Jesus as explained by his words.

Jesus is the revealer of God not so much through abstract discourses on the divinity as through the invitation he offers to the Jews and his disciples to gather from his everyday manner of life his personal relationship with the Father. Jesus desires to bring the disciples into his own interior life, into the kind of relationship that is his from eternity as the Son with the Father. All this is the divine reality that is offered to human beings and which only he who is always with the Father can communicate to humanity. The communion that is God's reality is made accessible to human beings in the sending of the incarnate Word.

It is also important to note that the revelation of God which Jesus communicates occurs essentially in the experience of an encounter. It is significant that the evangelist uses such expressions as "to show" the Father or "to see" the Father (see Jn 14:9-11); such phrases bring home to us the existential nature of revelation. Revelation takes place

---

13. John ends the episode of the wedding feast in Cana in this way: "Jesus performed the beginning of signs at Cana in Galilee and showed his glory, and his disciples believed in him" (2:11). The purpose of the first miracle, as of all the other "signs," is to reveal the glory of Jesus and thereby his divine origin.

not so much through the communication of truth as through the testimony of vision. The Prologue of the first Letter lays special emphasis on the visual, historical experience which the first witnesses had of the person of Jesus: "What was from the beginning, what we heard, what we saw with our eyes, what we contemplated and (what) our hands touched" (1 Jn 1:1, 2b, 3a).[14] It was their historical, physical seeing, but transformed into an interior knowledge of the reality seen, that the first disciples passed on to later generations, in order that these, too, might be able to "see" in faith.

In contemplation of the behavior of Jesus in his everyday life, the truth that dwells in him shines through. By revealing himself, he also makes the Father known. The evangelist is therefore able to sum up the entire mission of Jesus as "the manifesting of the Father," this being understood as the completion of his work (Jn 17:4, 6).

Let us now try to see in the gospel how Jesus revealed God to be a communion of persons.

3. Jesus by His Own Life Reveals God

Our starting point has to be the fundamental assertion made in the Prologue: Jesus is none other than the Word made man (v. 14), that is, the one who is eternally turned toward the bosom of the Father and who lives in a relationship of love and intimacy with the Father that constitutes him as Son.

---

14. See A. Dalbesio, *Quello che abbiamo udito e veduto* (Supplemento alla *Rivista Biblica*, 24; Bologna: EDB, 1990) 110-12.

The relation of Father and Son, which Jesus now makes manifest in his own earthly existence,[15] characterizes the pre-existence of the Word. It is in the light of this reality that the terms and expressions which the evangelist takes over from the tradition must be interpreted. Thus, when in the fourth gospel Jesus describes himself as "the one sent by the Father," he is not simply saying that God has given him a mission, as he does a prophet. Since the Word is pre-existent, when he is sent he leads others into the inner reality of his own existence with God: His mission is to make known the relationship which he has with the Father from eternity. This being so, his mission qualitatively transcends that of the greatest prophets, including the Messiah who was expected in Judaism.

It is no accident that to a greater extent than the other gospels the gospel of John uses the name "Son" in an unqualified sense. It is not simply a Christological title equivalent to "son of God," that is, the title which in the Old Testament signified a privileged relationship with YHWH in the carrying out of a specific role, and which was given to, for example, prophets or the king of Israel. In the fourth gospel, "Son" signifies the unique relationship which Jesus has with the Father from eternity; it is a term that henceforth has to do with the inner life of God. And it is this divine inner life that Jesus seeks to show to human beings by means of his behavior and his words.

From his first page on, John describes God not as a domineering and isolated sovereign, nor even as possessing

---

15. See R. Schnackenburg, *Jesus in the Gospels: A Biblical Christology* (St. Louisvill, KY: The Westminister John Knox Press 1995) 283ff.

the fatherhood that YHWH claims toward Israel, but in his relationship to the Son. In a context dealing with revelation, the evangelist writes:

He whom God has sent speaks the words of God,
because he (God) gives him the Spirit without
   measure.
The Father loves the Son
and has given everything into his hands.
(Jn 3:34-35)

John's purpose, in this setting of revelation, is to ground the authority of the Revealer's words and thereby the authenticity and definitive character of his teaching:

• Jesus is sent by God; therefore the words of Jesus are the words of the Father.[16]

• Jesus has received the Holy Spirit in its fullness from God,[17] and therefore his testimony is of a higher order than that of a prophet: His words have definitive value, because they are "Spirit and life" (Jn 6:63) and are able to bestow divine life.

• The Father has given everything into the hands of the Son. "The Semitic phrase 'to put something into the hands of another' means in general the conferring of power and authority."[18] The statement grounds the authority of the words of him whom God has sent and, more generally, the

---

16. The words recall the principle of the *Shaliah*: The one sent is as the one who sends him.

17. The context suggests this meaning for v. 34b; but another interpretation is also possible: Jesus gives the Spirit without measure to believers.

18. R. Schnackenburg, *The Gospel of John* 1, trans. K. Smyth (New York: Crossroad, 1982) 388.

unique power which Jesus, the one sent by God, has received for the sake of human beings.[19]

Of special interest is the statement in verse 35: "The
Father loves the Son," as the reason why the Son is given
everything for the sake of his saving work. "The love that
God has from eternity for his Son leads him also to entrust
to him everything on earth."[20] The love of the Father for
the Son is therefore the permanent foundation of the words
and actions of Jesus on earth.

R. Schnackenburg writes: "In terms of Christology, it
should be noted that the phrase does not speak of the
immanent self-communication of the Father to the Son
within the Trinity, but of the giving of knowledge and
power when the Son is sent as saviour." But the exegete
goes on to complete the thought: "Although on profounder
consideration the former appears to be the presupposition
of the fullness of knowledge and power communicated to
the Son."[21] In other words, when John writes these verses,
he has in mind the love with which the Father loves the Son
"before the creation of the world" (Jn 17:24) and which
characterizes him from eternity in his reality as Father.

In this light, great importance attaches to the expression
which we read in the final prayer of Jesus: "Preserve them
in your Name whom you have given to me." The totality
that the Son receives from the Father includes the "Name
of the Father." The statement is a strange one. What does

---

19. In the course of the gospel the "everything" that the Father gives to the
    Son is detailed: the Father's works that are to be done (5:36), the authority
    to judge (5:22, 27), life (5:26), believers (6:37, 39; 10:29; 17:2, 6, 9, 24;
    18:9), his words (17:8), his Name (17:11, 12), his glory (17:22, 24).
20. C. Spicq, *Agapè dans le Nouveau Testament* 3 (Paris: Gabalda, 1959) 135.
21. Schnackenburg, *The Gospel of John* 1:388.

it mean to say that Jesus, as Son, has received the Father's Name? "The Name given is the abiding revelation to the Son of the divine fatherhood that constitutes him in his being as Son. In revealing himself as Father, God gives himself entirely to the Son."[22]

The Father is thus revealed as "the love that gives everything" to the Son, as the One who lives his own divinity as a gift to the Son.

The evangelist takes up this theme again in the discussion of Jesus with the Jews after the cure of the paralytic at the pool of Beth-zatha. When he is accused of violating the law of the sabbath, Jesus replies: "My Father works always, and I too work" (Jn 5:17).

In the Synoptic gospels Jesus justifies cures worked on the sabbath by saying that "the Son of man is lord of the sabbath" (Mk 2:28), thereby placing the question on the level of discussion of the law. In John, however, the answer of Jesus "is on the level of God."[23] The action of Jesus on earth has its ultimate explanation in his life of communion with the Father.

The statement in John 5:17, which is still of a general kind, will be further spelled out in verse 19-20:

> Amen, amen, I say to you: Of himself the Son can do nothing, except what he sees the Father doing. Whatever he (the Father) does, the Son also does. In fact, the Father loves the Son and shows him everything that he is doing.

In verse 19 the subject is the Son, and the formulation

22. G. Rossé, *L'ultima preghiera di Gesù* (Rome: Città Nuova, 1988) 104.
23. Léon-Dufour, *Lettura* (note 6, above) 2:48.

starts out as a negative one. Jesus expresses an absolute and complete dependence on the Father, for he is by his nature always "turned toward the bosom of the Father" (1:18). The Son has, therefore, no initiative of his own and can do nothing by himself. The statement allows of no exception: The Son receives his very being from the Father, he possesses nothing that is not from the Father.

On the positive side, this means that whatever the Father does the Son also does or, inverting the two names, that whatever Jesus does the Father is also doing.

Verse 20 gives the ultimate reason for Jesus' claim and makes the Father the subject of the action. It repeats what had been said in John 3:5, except that a different Greek verb is used:[24] The Father loves the Son, opens himself completely to him, has no secrets from him. The Father "shows," the Son "looks/sees"; the reciprocity is constitutive of their being and action; the divine Persons receive themselves each from the other, and they act as one. This explains why the action of the Father is fulfilled in the action of Jesus. Jesus does not act alongside or after the action of the Father; rather the Father and the Son are one to the point that the action of the one is the action of the other.[25]

---

24. In 5:20 the evangelist uses the verb *philein*, and not *agapân* as in 3:35. Spicq, *Agapè* 3:220, sees a nuance of difference: 5:20 is referring to the love of friendship, of intimacy, that raises persons to the same level and creates reciprocity. On the other hand, S. A. Panimolli in his *Lettura pastorale del Vangelo di Giovanni* (2 vols.; Bologna: EDB, 1978-84) 2:41 and 71, thinks, perhaps rightly, that the two verbs are synonyms, as is shown by the use the evangelist makes of them elsewhere: the disciple whom Jesus loved (*agapân*: 13:23; 19:26); the disciple whom Jesus loved (*philein*: 20:2); and the love of Jesus for Lazarus is expressed by *philein* in 11:3 and by *agapân* in 11:5. See also 21:15-17.

25. See Schnackenburg, *The Gospel of John* 2, trans. C. Hastings et al. (New York: Crossroad, 1982) 104-5.

Such a union between Jesus and the Father can be explained, then, only by means of the utterly unparalleled relationship that the Son always has with the Father. Jesus' lack of his own initiative is not a limitation; rather it makes present, unveiled and with no shadow on it, the word and action of the Father. In this way Jesus lives and reveals his reality as Son and, at the same time, carries out his mission of making known the Father's Name (17:6). This implies the gift of a filial relationship for human beings.

As Son, Jesus receives everything from the Father, to the point where he cannot do anything on his own that is not also willed by the Father.[26] Jesus explains this to his disciples after the scene with the Samaritan woman: They urge him to take food, and he tells them: "I have a food to eat, of which you do not know" (4:32).

When the understanding of the disciples stops short at a purely material level ("Has someone perhaps brought him something to eat?"), Jesus explains: "My food is to do the will of him who sent me and to complete out his work" (4:34).

Here, as often elsewhere, John uses the device of misunderstanding in order to clarify what Jesus means. That is, the evangelist plays on the ambiguity or double meaning of words and attitudes in order to effect a passage from a material vision to a vision of faith. By doing so, he enables readers to distinguish the two levels clearly and to grasp what Jesus is saying in his revelatory discourse.

The life of the Son who is wholly turned to the Father is the response of love that Jesus gives to the Father. It is the doing of the Father's will that gives meaning to his entire

---

26. See the comment of J. Blank, *Das Evangelium nach Johannes* (4 vols.; Düsseldorf: Patmos, 1981) 2:22.

existence, and he is determined to do that will to the end, as the last part of 4:34 suggests: "to complete *his work.*" Thus, before handing himself over to death, Jesus can say: "I have completed the work you gave me to do" (17:4): the work to which his life was given over, namely, making known the Father's Name (17:6, 26).

Such is the program of Jesus, the choice on which his life is based and that fully reflects his own reality as Son. It is not an exceptional project aimed at putting himself forward and calling attention to himself, but rather the fulfillment of the will of an Other. He acknowledges and lives out his complete dependence on God, from whom his being and his existence receive their meaning.

The consciousness of doing not his own will but the will of the Father who sent him comes out in every section of the gospel.[27] It is for this reason that he has not come of his own will (8:42), does not speak on his own (12:49), does nothing on his own (8:28).

"Be it a question of *doing* or *saying* or *coming,* Jesus always says that none of it *comes from himself* but all from the Father. Is this not an echo of the Prologue: the only Son is turned toward the bosom of the Father (1:18)? Any claim of his own would hide the fact that in his actions it is the Father working on behalf of humanity."[28]

In order that the utterances and actions of Jesus may be a revelation of the word and working of the Father, Jesus must be completely open to the Father, to the point of himself being in a state of "nonbeing," that is, of being the

---

27. See 5:30; 6:38; 7:16-17; 8:28, 42; 12:49; 14:10.
28. Léon-Dufour, *Lettura* 2:61.

Son who receives his entire self from the Father. In this attitude of "nonbeing" which allows him to be the Son, Jesus is the transparent reflection of the Father.

We understand now that the work Jesus must complete on earth is not limited to a few signs, a few miracles, but is his *very existence* insofar as he is permanently directed to the Father, as the Word is eternally directed to the Father. Jesus makes known the Name, that is, the person of the Father, by living out in the midst of humanity his very existence as the Son. He makes this reality known in his daily obedience to the Father's will. Obedience does not, however, mean the blind carrying out of duties dictated by a boss; Jesus is not a passive doer of someone else's will, nor does his "nonbeing" signify a loss of personhood.

The work of Jesus is the work of the Father, but at the same time it is his own work, to which he commits all of his energies and for which he accepts full responsibility. It is *"the work you entrusted to me* that I might do it."[29] "Far from simply ordering the Son to execute his will, the Father *gives* him his (the Father's) work so that it may also be his own. The Father's work, received as a gift, has become the Son's project as well."[30] *By being himself, Jesus expresses the Father.*

He can therefore say that he is never alone because "he who sent me is with me; he has not left me alone, for I do always what is pleasing to him" (8:29; see 8:16). The work Jesus accomplishes on earth is the fruit of a joint action of the Father and the Son. Jesus is never alone; for this reason,

---

29. Translation of 5:17c by A. Vanhoye, in *Recherches de science religieuse* 48 (1960) 377ff.
30. Léon-Dufour, *Lettura* 1:507.

believers never meet Jesus apart from the Father, nor the Father apart from Jesus.

John sums up the divine reality made known by Jesus in the pregnant formula: "I and the Father are one" (10:30). Their oneness is such that, as was said above, the words and works of the one are the words and works of the other. Nevertheless, the evangelist always safeguards the distinction between the persons: "However close and indissoluble the union of the Father and the Son (and of the Son and believers), it is never a fusion but a communion."[31]

We are now in a position to grasp the revelation of God that John wants to give to the readers of his work. He is not describing the attributes of a monolithic divinity that is closed in on itself and situated beyond the reach of human beings. Jesus makes known a God who is in reality a communion. What becomes visible in his words and deeds is the interior dynamics of the divine oneness, which is a dialogue of love,[32] in which the Father manifests himself as Father by giving everything, and in which the Son is himself in a complete openness to the Father.

4. Jesus Reveals God in His Own Death

The revelation of God reaches its climax in the crucified Jesus, and it is not surprising that John describes the death of Jesus not only in relation to the salvation of humankind but also as a part of the relationship of love between Father and Son:

---

31. Ibid., 2:493.
32. The Father's love for the Son: 3:35; 5:20; 10:17; 15:9; 17:23; the Son's love for the Father: 14:31.

This is why the Father loves me:
because I lay down my life in order
to take it up again.[33]
No one takes it from me, but I lay it down
of my own accord.
I have the power to lay it down
and I have the power to take it up again.
That is the command I have received from my Father.
(Jn 10:17-18)

There is here the paradox of a complete submission of the Son to the Father's command and, at the same time, the complete freedom of the Son to give and take back his own life. The seeming contradiction is resolved only in the light of the perfect communion between Father and Son.

In dying, Jesus does the work of the Father in the most personal act of his own existence. "It is the moment in which the action of Christ is in complete accord with the action of the Father."[34]

John interprets in his own way the verb *dei* ("it is necessary") which the synoptic gospels apply to the death of Jesus (see Mk 8:31 and par.): It states that his death is the manifestation of the Father's love for the Son, a love that, through the Son's free decision to die, will achieve the

---

33. In Johannine theology the expression "lay down one's life in order to take it up again" does not render the death of Jesus less serious, as though it were simply a pleasant passing. Rather, the death and resurrection are seen as a single event (see the words "when I shall be lifted up . . . ," in 8:28; 12:32); the resurrection is the completion of his death. Jesus rises in death, not after death; see R. E. Brown, *The Gospel according to John* (2 vols.; Anchor Bible 29 and 29A; Garden City, NY: Doubleday, 1966 and 1970) 1:399.

34. Cilia, *La morte di Gesù* (note 9, above) 128.

glorification of both the Son and the Father. In the crucified Jesus the Trinity reveals the splendor of its own life.

> Glorify the Son in order
> that the Son may glorify you.
> (Jn 17:1)

The reciprocal glorification at the moment of the "hour"—a moment now being lived out in eternity[35]—expresses perfectly that which has arisen out of the life of Jesus and which the paschal mystery makes known: the splendor of the relationship of Father and Son, in which each of these Persons receives himself in the gift and acceptance of the other, and each is established in his own place. It is the splendor of the divine intimacy, manifesting itself to humanity.

Four times (3:14; 8:28; 12:32, 34) John uses the verb *hypsoun* (raise up, lift on high) in connection with the death of Jesus, and he exploits its entire semantic riches.[36] The verb describes the physical action of lifting up on a stake, and therefore the crucifixion; but it also expresses the deeper meaning of that action as perceived by faith: the exaltation of Jesus and, more specifically, his crowning as king. Unlike the Acts of the Apostles, for example, in which the exaltation of Jesus is identified with his ascension, John connects the royal exaltation of Jesus directly with the cross, which is for him the place of supreme revelation.

The first of the four passages listed already stresses the

---

35. "In the term 'glorify' John has created a linguistic instrument which brings under a particular concept the whole of Jesus' saving work, as it continues and is completed in the action of Christ with God through the Spirit, in the disciples" (Schnackenburg, *The Gospel according to John* 2:402).

36. See Cilia, *La morte di Gesù*, 99ff.

sign value of the cross; it is the place where salvation is accomplished:

> As Moses lifted up the serpent in the wilderness
> (see Nm 21:8-9; Wis 16:7),
> so the Son of man must be lifted up,
> so that everyone who believes may have eternal life
> through him. (Jn 3:14)

In John's eyes, the cross, which was a sign of disgrace and shame in the ancient world, must be gazed upon and contemplated (see Jn 9:37), but, as Cilia writes, "the gaze must not stop at the suffering and death of Jesus, but must go on to see in the suffering and dying Jesus the saving action of God, the work that the Father is bringing to completion in Jesus and that Jesus, too, is bringing to completion by his death."[37] The saving action on behalf of those who believe is in turn inseparable from the revelation of God that is given by the crucified Jesus. Looking at the cross, the gaze of faith discovers the identity of Jesus:

> When you have lifted up the Son of man,
> then you shall know that I am:
> I do nothing on my own,
> but as the Father has taught me, so I speak.
> He who sent me is with me
> and has not left me alone,
> because I do always the things
> that are pleasing to him.
> (Jn 8:28-30)

---

37. Ibid., 104.

The identity of Jesus is here expressed in the unqualified "I am" formula, which in John's language signifies the divinity of Jesus. The very fact of being lifted up on the cross reveals not only the divinity of Jesus but also the sense in which Jesus is God: He does nothing by himself and speaks the words of the Father, not his own. When lifted up, he does not, then, reveal a second God alongside God; if we look at him with the eyes of faith, we discover a single God in a communion of Persons. The true identity of Jesus can therefore be known only by those who recognize his oneness with the Father, those who make their way through the crucified Jesus into the very inner being of God, and, consequently, only by those who realize that the entire existence and mission of Jesus have been at every point a revelation of the Father by the Son who makes the Father visible. The Father has indeed never left the Son alone; he has always been with him, and especially at the crowning moment of his work, on the cross.

The early tradition, which is accepted by Mark and Matthew, sees Jesus dying in isolation and expressing his sense of abandonment by God. The fourth gospel, on the other hand, sees the cross as the moment that sheds the clearest light on the oneness of Jesus with the Father. Is John then contradicting the early Christian tradition? No, he is in fact simply explaining to the reader the true meaning of Jesus' death as seen by faith: This death, this immense loneliness are in reality the crowning point of the revelation of God, the point at which the Son shows his supreme oneness with the Father.[38]

---

38. We may not exclude the possibility that in verse 29 John meant to respond to an erroneous interpretation of Jesus' cry of abandonment.

The theme of Jesus lifted up occurs again in his last public action (Jn 12:23-36). When lifted up on the cross as king, he will dethrone the one who leads the world astray, and he will exert a universal drawing power:

> Now the prince of this world will be cast out.
> When I am lifted up on the cross,
> I will draw all (human beings) to myself.
> (Jn 12:31b-32)[39]

The evangelist here brings out a further aspect of the death of Jesus: When lifted up, he will draw all to himself, with the intention of establishing a communion with those who look beneath the surface and allow themselves to be drawn.

John had earlier used the verb "draw" (*helkoun*) in the discourse on the bread of life, in a passage in which the subject of the action was the Father. This earlier use will help shed light on our present passage:

> No one can come to me,
> unless the Father who sent me draws him.
> It is written in the prophets:
> "And all will be taught by God."
> Whoever has listened to the Father
> and has learned from him comes to me.
> Not that anyone has seen the Father,
> but only the one who comes from God

---

39. On Jn 12:32 and 11:51-52, see I. de la Potterie, "L'esaltazione del figlio dell'uomo (Gv 12, 31-36)," in his *Gesù verità* (note 2, above) 85ff.; see also Cilia, *La morte di Gesù.*

Jesus crucified fulfills the promise made to the Servant of Yahweh in Isaiah 52—53: "He shall be exalted, lifted up. . . . I will give him the multitudes as his inheritance" (Isa 52:13 and 53:12).

has seen the Father.
(Jn 6:44, 45-46)

In the new covenant, as the scriptures foretold (see Jer 31:33-34), the Father himself becomes the teacher of human beings. But his teaching directs them to Jesus and not to the Father himself, as we might have expected.

As always, John deliberately stresses the initiative of the Father, which is exercised in everything, just as he does also the indispensable mediation of Christ.

Verse 46 helps make the matter clear and prevents any contradiction with the statement in John 12:32, where it is Jesus himself who takes the initiative. The evangelist here repeats the dominant theme of the Prologue (Jn 1:18): Only the incarnate Son has seen the Father. Consequently, and inevitably, the attraction exercised by the Father is exercised through Jesus, for the latter alone is the revealer. We know that the words of Jesus are the words of the Father; when we attend and listen to the words of Jesus, who makes the Father known, it is the Father himself who draws the hearts of the listeners to the revealer, who speaks the Father's words.

"For disciples, to learn from the Father means to welcome the revelation of Jesus by acknowledging him, by faith, as the one sent by the Father, the one who speaks the words of God."[40]

If everything comes from the Father, then the final movement is in turn a movement toward the Father, but always through Jesus.

---

40. Cilia, *La morte di Gesù*, 116. The Paraclete is also a teacher (see Jn 14:25f.). The Holy Spirit teaches by conveying the deeper meaning of the words of Jesus; he does not speak words different from those of Jesus, but interiorizes these in the believer (Jn 16:12-14).

Returning to John 12:32, we can say that the crucified Jesus draws to himself because, thanks to the Spirit given to them, believers contemplate in the one lifted up the Son who is eternally turned toward the Father. But the identity of Jesus is inseparable from his oneness with the Father (see 8:28-29), and so it is in his obedience to the end that his revelation of the Father reaches its climax. The drawing by the Father, then, is accomplished when Jesus, too, draws; that is, at the moment when he most fully reveals the Father. At the supreme moment of his love for the Father, Jesus allows the Father's love for humanity to shine through fully (see 3:16) and, by drawing believers to himself, takes them into the relationship which he, the Son, has eternally with the Father within the Trinity.

Once again, then, the close relationship of Father and Son is the ultimate explanation of the drawing of humanity by both the Father and the Son: "My Father works always, and I, too, work" (5:17). In the work of salvation there is a perfect collaboration of the divine Persons, so that those who come to know this work always encounter the trinitarian reality of God.[41]

The attraction which Jesus exerts on human beings as the one lifted up has a very particular purpose: It leads into the divine unity.

---

41. I use the term "trinitarian," a concept which derives from a later theology, because I think it corresponds to the Johannine vision of God as a communion of Persons even if the evangelist never clearly formulates a trinitarian doctrine. That is, the evangelist does not develop the Holy Spirit's role in the intimacy of the Godhead. For the "Johannine school," the Paraclete is a divine Person (not solely an attribute of God) that has a relationship with the Father and with the Son that he communicates to believers (cf. Jn 14:16; 15:26; 16:7, 13-15). All that we find written about the Holy Spirit in the Johannine works supports the later theological conclusions.

John develops this theme in 11:49-52, on the occasion of Caiaphas' sentence, which seemingly only applies "nationalist considerations" to the case of Jesus, that is, the principle that an individual's life may be taken if this serves the common cause.

But the evangelist interprets Caiaphas' words as a prophecy; he finds in them a deeper meaning that relates to God's plan, and he explains it as follows:

> Jesus had to die for the nation,
> and not for the nation alone,
> but also to bring together into unity (*synagein eis hen*)
> the scattered children of God.
> (11:51-52)

The phrase "bring . . . unity" is again connected with the present theme in the prayer of Jesus: the expectation that God will once again bring together the scattered people of Israel. John is saying that through the crucified Jesus the situation of dispersal, which for the evangelist signifies non-communion with God,[42] is overcome: Jesus dies "to bring together into unity the scattered children of God."

It is true, of course, that the evangelist gives the words a particular reference of his own: He is thinking of believers who have come from Judaism and of converts from the non-Jewish world. But, to shed light on the theme with which I am dealing, I would like rather to dwell on the expression "bring together into unity," in which the words "into unity" translate the Greek *eis hen*.

---

42. See Cilia, *La morte di Gesù*, 71.

The Greek expression can be translated as "gather together," meaning "to form a universal people"; in this interpretation, *eis hen* would simply intensify the meaning already present in "bring together."

But *eis hen* can have a more pregnant meaning and describe a movement (*eis*) toward a place (*hen*). That is, the children of God are being led to a place, namely, unity; in other words, the place in which believers gather together is the relationship between Father and Son,[43] the pre-existing unity of the divine Persons into which the children of God can be brought.[44] For John, in fact, "there is no unity except that of the Father and the Son; outside this unity there is only dispersal."[45]

Jesus, then, leads humanity into the "temple"—himself—in which the Father and the Son are one. Cilia suggests therefore the following translation: Jesus had to die "in order to reunite the children of God, the scattered, by leading them into unity." He goes on to explain why he prefers the abstract word "unity" to the more correct "one" (*hen*):

Because in 11:52 the author [John] does not intend primarily to describe the unique bond between the Son and the Father, but to say that thanks to the death of Jesus believers can be brought by him into the vital space constituted by the relationship between Father and Son, and thereby share, in Jesus, in

43. The relationship between Father and Son is expressed by the neuter *hen* ("a single thing") in Jn 10:30 and 17:22.
44. See Cilia, *La morte di Gesù*, 82.
45. Ibid., 83.

the dynamic unity and attraction that binds him to the Father.[46]

On the basis of John's explanation in 11:52, it is possible also to explain better the statement in 12:32: Jesus draws to himself the human beings who allow themselves to be drawn, because he brings them into himself as into a temple; in him they will find communion with God by sharing in the relationship of Jesus with the Father.

Only initiation into the divine unity makes possible unity among human beings.

Jesus lifted up thus brings to completion his work on earth: He is the center of revelation because of his oneness with the Father; he is the center of attraction because he brings the children of God together into unity in himself; and he is the holy place of unity because he introduces them all into the divine intimacy of his own oneness with the Father.

5. Conclusion: The Vocation of the Human Being

In the light of the post-Easter faith (see Jn 2:22), which is taught by the Spirit who leads us "into the entire truth" (Jn 16:13), that is, into a life-giving understanding of Jesus as the one sent by the Father, the evangelist contemplates the historical Jesus and reflects on his behavior in relation to his Father. This behavior reveals the intimate, eternal relationship between the Father and the Son.

John has simply clarified and gone more deeply into what the Christian tradition was passing on.

---

46. Ibid., 89.

The dominant theme that runs through the fourth gospel derives from both the central tradition of Israel and the new reality of Christianity:

• No one can see God and thus know him in his innermost life (Jn 1:18; 5:37; 6:46).

• Only Jesus, the incarnate Word who lives with the Father, knows him and is therefore able to reveal him.

• He reveals the Father by revealing himself as Son; this is his life's work.

• By living in accordance with the Father's will in an obedience that has its climax on the cross, Jesus allows the Father to be seen fully.

• Jesus lifted up is the center of revelation: On the cross he manifests the supreme divine unity that opens itself up to humanity and the love of the Father, who gives his only-begotten Son for the salvation of the world (see Jn 3:16; 15:13).

• When believers draw near to Jesus, they encounter not one person but a "we"; in this "we" the divine persons manifest themselves in their intimate being and introduce human beings into the dynamic dialogue of love between the "I" and the divine "Thou."

The basic theme is summarized in John 14:2-11, which everyone regards as the climactic point in the Johannine theology of salvation.

After speaking, with an eye to the future, of the destination promised to the disciples, namely, that they will be alongside Jesus with the Father (vv. 2-4), the discourse turns back to the present and takes up the theme of the way for reaching the Father:

Thomas says to him:
"Lord, we do not know where you are going,
how can we know the way?"
Jesus says to him:
"I am the way and the truth and the life;
no one comes to the Father except through me,
If you had known me, you would also know
      my Father;
and now you already know him and have seen him."
Philip says to him:
"Lord, show us the Father, and it is enough for us!"
Jesus says to him:
"I have been with you for so long,
and you do not know me, Philip?
Whoever sees me, sees the Father.
How can you say: 'Show us the Father'?
Do you not believe
that I am in the Father and the Father is in me?
The words I speak to you I do not speak on my own.
The Father who dwells in me is doing his works.
Believe me: I am in the Father and the Father
      is in me.
Believe at least because of these works."
(Jn 14:5-11)

As is his custom, the evangelist uses the device of a
misunderstanding—in this case, that of Thomas and
Philip—as a literary means of developing the discourse on
revelation and making its meaning clear to the reader.

Jesus' response begins with the proclamation of a truth
that is universal in scope: The man Jesus is henceforth the

way that leads to the Father, because he is the truth and therefore also the life (v. 6a).[47]

Since Jesus is, in himself, the revelation of the Father—that is, "the Truth"—and possesses the Father's Life in its fullness, he is the Way that leads to the Father. In these few words John sums up his teaching on salvation as based entirely on Jesus, and at the same time he asserts that the goal of the human vocation is the Father.

Jesus is therefore the sole mediator (v. 6b). "The man Jesus is in our midst as the living epiphany of the Father."[48]

He is now in a position to answer Thomas' question: "How can we know the way?" (v. 5). Given that Jesus is in himself the way, to know him is to know the Father (v. 7).

In the world of the Bible "to know" does not signify simply to grasp intellectually; it implies entering into a communion, having a relationship of intimacy with a person (see Jn 15:15).[49] The disciple is already, here and

---

47. See I. de la Potterie, "Io sono la Via, la Verità e la Vita," in his *Studi di Cristologia giovannea* (Genoa: Marietti, 1986) 124ff.

    In the Greek text the three words are co-ordinates and can therefore be translated in various ways:

    1) "I am the Way that leads to the Truth which is Life": the Truth, which is identical with the divine essence, is the goal to be reached (this is the Platonizing interpretation of the Alexandrian Fathers).

    2) "I am the Way that leads through the Truth to Life": The goal is life, and truth is the means to it. But this reading does not take into account that in the text of John Jesus is the way to the Father, not to life.

    3) "I am the Way because I am the Truth and therefore also Life." Truth and Life are explained by the fact that Jesus is the Way that leads to the Father. This is the interpretation to be preferred (see Léon-Dufour, *Lettura* 3:126ff.).

48. de la Potterie, "Io sono la Via," 153.

49. In his article "*Oida e Ghinôskô*. I due modi del 'conoscere' nel quarto Vangelo" (*Studi di Cristologia giovannea*, 303ff.), I. de la Potterie has shown that the verb *ghinôskein* ("to know") usually signifies the acquisition of knowledge, not its finished possession (which is expressed by *oida*, "I know"). The verb "know," then, implicitly contains the idea of growth or progress in knowledge (see Jn 8:22; 15:7s.).

now,[50] living in this kind of communion with Jesus. Consequently, Philip, in his relationship with Jesus, is already living in a relationship of intimacy with the Father.

When Philip asks, "Lord, show us the Father," he wants to attain, thanks to Jesus, to that to which knowledge of God is tending: to the direct vision of God, which only the incarnate Word possesses (see Jn 6:46). The request is reminiscent of that of Moses: "Show me your glory!" (Ex 33:18); perhaps Philip is asking for a theophany like that for which Moses asked and which would remove any doubts he had.

But Philip "spoke as if Jesus and the Father were *two* and Jesus were simply an intermediary and not the Mediator in the full sense of the word."[51] Philip represents a temptation often experienced by Christians: "Jesus' criticism of Philip . . . warns them [later believers] not to look for special visionary experiences of God or any form of direct union with God, but to be content simply to believe in Jesus and his words."[52]

Jesus repeats what he said to the crowd in John 12:45: To see Jesus is to see the Father. The visibility of the Father is based on the perfect unity which Jesus, as Son, has with the Father from eternity and which the evangelist expresses in his formula of reciprocal immanence: "I am in the Father,

---

50. In v. 7a there is a textual variant in the tense of the verbs. Some manuscripts have: "If you had known me, you would also have known the Father"; this sounds like a rebuke that is hardly in harmony with the context. The reading to be preferred is therefore: "If you knew me, you would also know the Father," with Jesus referring to the time he has spent on earth with his disciples. Along the same lines, *ap'arti* (v. 7b) is to be translated as "now" or "already" and not as "henceforth."

51. Léon-Dufour, *Lettura*, 3:132.

52. Schnackenburg, *The Gospel according to John* 3:69.

and the Father is in me" (vv. 10, 11). Because of this reciprocal indwelling the Father works in the works of Jesus; these works manifest the intimate communion between the Son and the Father in the bosom of the trinitarian life. Disciples are therefore called to "see," with their bodily eyes, the man Jesus and his way of acting. But this seeing must be transcended in an interior seeing by faith, in order that it may open into the mystery of the person of the Son and his eternal union with the Father. Thus only the bodily seeing of the disciple can become a testimony and a tradition that enable future generations as well to believe and to see (see Jn 20:29; 1 Jn 1:1-3).

Since Jesus is the incarnate Word, he is the only Mediator able to make the Father known and seen, and he is this in two ways: in a descending movement, as revealer of the Father, and in an ascending movement, as way to the Father.[53]

Furthermore, as Mediator, Jesus is not simply a stage in the passage to the Father, as if the encounter with the Father came after that stage. Communion with the Father is always understood as taking the form of a relationship as son or daughter and therefore in a total adherence to Jesus, in a being *in* Christ as in the holy place where God is present. Jesus himself, in his transparent existence as Son, makes the Father directly present. Communion with God is never a static relationship with a divine person; it is life within the trinitarian love.

The cross is not merely the climax of revelation; it also accomplishes the saving purpose of the incarnation of the Word, precisely insofar as it is a lifting up and an exaltation. Revelation and salvation are closely connected from the

53. de la Potterie, *Studi di Cristologia giovannea*, 150.

viewpoint of the fourth gospel. In his obedience to the end, the man Jesus reaches full union with the Father, that is, the completion, in his humanity, of his relationship as Son at the moment when he freely surrenders his life out of love for human beings. This is the "drawing" movement that has as its result the gathering of the dispersed into unity (see 11:52) and that makes it possible, thanks to the gift of the Holy Spirit, for human beings to be brought into his life as Son within the Trinity.[54]

John sees this salvation symbolized by the blood and water that come from the side of the crucified Jesus (Jn 19:34f.): the blood, which signifies the gift of life and therefore the "greater love" (Jn 15:13); the water, which is a sign of the communication of the Holy Spirit. I borrow here the thoughts of Cilia:

> By giving the Spirit, Jesus gives a share in his own life, that of the Son, which he has brought to its end and goal by surrendering it in obedience to the Father's will and out of love for the disciples. In light of this, the pair of symbols, blood and water, takes on their meaning, as does the order of the two: first, the blood, then the water. The outpouring of the Holy Spirit is the fruit borne by the gift of his life, which Jesus has made in obedience to the Father and out of love for humanity, and of which the blood is the symbol. The purpose of the outpouring is to communicate the life of Jesus himself. Thanks to the gift of the Spirit to those who can look upon and believe in the one who was pierced, it is possible, in communion with Jesus, to participate

---

54. See Cilia, *La morte di Gesù*, 133f.

in the filial relationship that unites Jesus the Son with the Father (see especially 14:1-28), and therefore to be filled with the same dynamism that led Jesus to live his life in fulfillment of the Father's will and out of love for humanity. (15:12-13)[55]

The relationship between the Father and the Son, then, does not unfold in a closed circle. In the incarnate Son, God has opened himself to humanity and urges human beings to enter into his own inner life to share in the movement of the love of the divine persons, and to live the life of unity even among themselves (see Jn 11:52; 17:21ff.).

Such is the human-divine calling of the community of human beings. John sums it up in the words of the prayer for unity:

This is eternal life,
that they know you, the only true God,
and the one you sent, Jesus Christ.
(Jn 17:3)[56]

Given the meaning of the verb "to know," the evangelist is able to describe eternal life as consisting in a knowledge of God, or, in other words, as a participation in the life of communion of the divine persons. In the present time, believers who are obedient to the message of Jesus already

---

55. Ibid., 130.

56. Some of the phrases suggest that this verse may be a gloss added by the Johannine School: "the only true God" recalls the monotheistic acclamation (see 1 Thes 1:9) of the synagogue and the Church; the expression "Jesus Christ" is not common in John and is unexpected in a prayer uttered by Jesus himself. The thought, however, is indeed Johannine.

possess this "eternal life"; here on earth they are living their life of mutual love within the Trinity.

Communion with God, participation in the divine *koinônia* that exists from eternity between the Father and the Son: Such is the goal of the work of Jesus, which is also the Father's work. Such, too, then, is the way of salvation and the ultimate purpose of human life.

This vocation is clearly affirmed again in the first Letter of John, in which the idea of "communion with God and with Jesus Christ" serves as an inclusion[57] for the entire document (1 Jn 1:3 and 5:20).[58]

The conclusion to be drawn is then an obvious one: Jesus reveals God to be a communion of persons; he dies in order to bring human beings together into unity. He certainly does not offer an individualistic spirituality to anyone who accepts his revelation! If the dispersed who are gathered together are brought into the intimacy of the divine communion, then Christian spirituality can only be a spirituality of communion that is a reflection of the trinitarian spiritual life.

The life of communion that should characterize Christian life has its ultimate foundation in God himself, who reveals himself to be a communion of persons.

---

57. An inclusion is a stylistic device that consists in repeating at the end of a passage a word or expression or ideas that occurs at the beginning of the passage, thus creating a literary unit.

58. In 1 John 1:3 "God and Jesus Christ" are coordinated by the word *kai* ("and"); in 5:20 the phrase "in his Son Jesus Christ" stands in apposition to "him," i.e., God. In both instances the relation between Father and Son is not one simply of mediation (we go to the Father through the Son) but also one of communion: the mutual gift of Father and Son. To express mediation John uses the preposition *dia* ("through, by means of"); see Jn 14:6b.

Chapter 2

The Human Response: Faith

The revelation brought by Jesus is, then, not so much a communication of truths as it is a communication of his very self in his relationship with the Father and an invitation to human beings to enter into this divine intimacy.

What should be the human response to this invitation? John reduces it to two basic activities that are closely connected with one another: believing and loving. He gives this summary in 1 John 3:23:

> And this is his commandment:
> that we believe in the Name of his Son Jesus Christ
> and that we love one another
> according to the commandment that he gave us.[1]

Such a description of the whole Christian life as one of faith and love is typical of a spirituality of communion.

---

1. The fact that the evangelist lists the two requirements, faith and love, as a single commandment (the Greek word *entolê* is in singular in number) shows that he regards them as closely connected, although not identical: in fact, faith calls for actions (see the same connection in Gal 5:6); the present study will show that the connection is, theologically, even deeper.

1. Faith in Relation to Revelation

The purpose the evangelist sets himself is to bring men and women to faith, as is clear from the first ending of the gospel (Jn 20:30-31). This is in fact the basic theme that runs through the gospel, especially in its first part (chapters 1–12).

Faith in Jesus is what God really wills; it is his great and urgent invitation to human beings, the new but absolutely necessary step that is required of them and that renders inadequate any other kind of effort to seek God. When the Jews ask Jesus what they must do in order to do "the works of God," that is, to do what pleases God, he answers: "This is the work of God: to believe in the one whom he has sent" (Jn 6:28f.). In place of zeal for the Torah ("works"), the evangelist proposes a single requirement: faith in the one sent; *that* is the response that pleases God. With the coming of Jesus one period of history has made way for another:

> The Law was given through Moses;
> grace and truth have come through Jesus Christ.
> (Jn 1:17)

John does not oppose Law and faith (see 5:45-47). The Law was a gift of God, but it is now transcended by the gift of Truth, that is, by the definitive fullness of revelation which only Jesus, the incarnate Word, can communicate (see 1:18). Jesus is the complete and unexpected fulfillment of what Jews expected from observance of the Law. But this new reality offends faithful Jews: the man Jesus, whose parents and place of birth people know (Jn 6:42; see 7:27,

41f.), is the pre-existent Son in whom God has definitively revealed himself!

In John's understanding of it, an act of faith is an act of complete, personal attachment to Christ[2] and a commitment by which one binds oneself to him in a radical way. It is an act that involves the entire person of the believer. Such an act contains the elements of biblical faith: trust, fidelity, the gift of self to God, bearing witness, a commitment to carry out his will.[3]

In addition, "to believe" implies listening, being converted, seeing and contemplating, an intellectual grasp and the kind of knowing that is a communion, and action. Faith thus engages the will but also the spiritual senses of the human being.[4]

Faith is a vital, dynamic reality that involves the whole of a person's existence and therefore implies a process of maturation, a journey of growth. It also implies the possibility of trials and crises to be surmounted.

---

2. It is to be noted that in the gospel of John, which uses the verb "to believe" (*pisteuein*) a good 96 times, the noun "faith" (*pistis*) is completely absent (this noun occurs only once, in 1 John). It is obvious that in the evangelist's understanding of it faith is something dynamic, existential, and not a state or a doctrine. John uses the verb in various ways:
    —*pisteuein* + *hoti* = "to believe that," that is, to accept a truth about a person, who in this case is Jesus (13 times).
    —*pisteuein* + the dative case (indirect object), "to believe someone," that is, to respond with faith to the testimony given by someone (18 times).
    —*pisteuein* + *eis* + accusative case: "to believe in(to)," that is, believing as a movement that brings someone to Jesus. This is the most frequent use (36 times).
    —*pisteuein* by itself occurs 30 times, with several meanings, ranging from "to become a Christian" all the way to "have faith" in the full Johannine sense.

3. See R. Schnackenburg, *Die sittliche Botschaft des Neuen Testaments* (2 vols.; Freiburg i. B.: Herder, 1988) 2:160ff.

4. See A. Dalbesio, *Quello che abbiamo udito e veduto* (Bologna: Edizioni Dehoniane, 1990) 137ff.

In the fourth gospel, when the verb *believe* is used absolutely, that is, without any complement, it often signifies faith understood as this kind of all-embracing reality.[5]

Let me now turn to faith in its relation to the subject of the present study. In a way that is fully consistent with his theological vision, the evangelist regularly connects "believe" with revelation. He thinks of faith, not as an acceptance of the proclamation of the death and resurrection of Jesus and of its salvific value (this is the heart of the apostolic preaching, or kerygma), but as an opening of the self to the revelation of God in Jesus.

To believe, then, consists in acknowledging and accepting the mystery of the person of Jesus. In the act of believing there is a passage from a strictly physical seeing and touching to a spiritual understanding.[6] Human beings are thus urged to learn how to look, how to *see* in the man Jesus the divine dimension; to discover his deeper identity and thus his reality as the Son sent by the Father, the only revealer capable of communicating to human beings the inner reality of God as a communion of persons that has opened itself to receive humanity.

Obviously, this act of attachment to Christ does not exclude the intellectual aspect of knowledge, but it does establish a vital bond with Christ; it advances to a kind of

---

5. Jn 1:7; 3:15, 18; 4:41, 53; 6:47; etc.

6. See 1 Jn 1:1-3. The seeing and touching of the historical, visible Jesus was absolutely necessary for the disciples who were the contemporaries of Jesus, just as was the kind of seeing that went beyond the bodily senses. This enabled them to become witnesses to and authentic transmitters of the tradition; in the presence of this last, later generations are likewise called upon to move from a material understanding of it to a vision of faith. Clearly, in this passage it is God who, through the Spirit, acts in human beings.

knowledge that is a full communion with Jesus and, in him, with the Father.

2. Faith in Jesus

As we have seen, John emphasizes the Christological dimension of the act of faith. The stress is placed, not on "believing in God," but on "believing in Jesus Christ."[7]
The importance that John assigns to the relationship of the believer with Christ can already be seen in the frequency with which the verb *believe* is followed, in the Greek text, by *eis* + the accusative case, with this complement being "Jesus" in the great majority of instances. This means that faith is essentially directed to him. The evangelist makes this clear in, for example, the cure of the man born blind, a cure that is located, not by accident, in the context of Jesus' statement: "I am the light of the world" (8:12). In this account, the reader is present at the birth of a faith that places the man in communion with the Light, after he had been blind from birth. The man whose sight has been restored becomes aware, first of all, of "the man called Jesus" (9:11); then he says: "He is a prophet" (9:17); he then recognizes that this man is from God (9:33); and finally, in a personal encounter with Jesus, he reaches full faith in him as the Son of Man (9:38). John makes us present to the birth and the gradual development of a faith that reaches its term when the man realizes who Jesus is and attaches himself to him with his entire being.

---

7. Here we find a characteristic Johannine phrasing: *pisteuein* + *eis* + the accusative. Only in John 14:1 does *pisteuein eis* have God as its complement.

In expressing the Christological direction taken by faith, the evangelist sometimes uses other words and phrases that are substantially synonyms of "believe": "to receive/accept Jesus" (1:12; 5:43; 13:20); "to go/come to Jesus" (5:40; 6:35, 37, 44f., 65); "to follow Jesus" (1:37f.; 4:44; 8:12; 10:4, 5, 27); "to love Jesus" (8:42; 14:15, 21, 23, 28; 16:27).

It is worth reflecting, in this context, on the formula of reciprocal immanence, which the evangelist uses in order to underscore the very close union between Jesus and believers.

In John 10, by way of comment on the parable of the Good Shepherd, who "calls his sheep one by one," and of the sheep that "know his voice" (vv. 3-4), the evangelist writes:

> I am the good shepherd, I know my sheep
> and my sheep know me,
> as the Father knows me
> and I know the Father.
> (Jn 10:14-15a)

We know that in John the verb "to know" implies a personal relationship of communion and expresses a deep-going bond of trust and love.[8] The close relationship be-

---

8. In the world of the Bible and Judaism, "to know God" includes the following aspects:
  —The gift of self to Yahweh by a life in conformity with the requirements of the covenant.
  —The practice of mercy, justice, and fidelity.
  —A personal encounter with God through knowledge of his plan, through creation, and through the gift of the word and of the divine Spirit, both of which are communicated to us.
  On the part of Yahweh, "to know Israel" implies making it the object of his election and concern, entering into a communion of life with his people, and testing them. See N. Lazure, *Les Valeurs morales de la Théologie johannique* (Paris: Gabalda, 1965) 221f.

tween a shepherd and his sheep has as its model and basis[9] the very relationship that exists between the Son and the Father. As I. de la Potterie remarks: "Living as they do in communion with Jesus and with what is deepest in him, believers are in communion with the Son of God and, by that fact, enter into the life-giving communion that unites the Son and the Father; they themselves also become children of God."[10]

Because, then, of their close union with Christ, believers come to share in the communion between Jesus and the Father. In the allegory of the vine and the branches John brings home to us how close and life-giving our union with Jesus is: As in the vine the one sap flows from the trunk into the branches, so too with Jesus and believers.

It is not by chance that the formula of reciprocal immanence occurs in varied forms and with some frequency in the allegory of the vine and the branches (vv. 4, 5, 7) and that the expression "remain in" is emphasized. The allegory confirms that the intention of the formula is to convey a relationship of identity at the level of living, while firmly maintaining a radical distinction. The believer is united to Jesus, and Jesus to the believer, so that the latter is given a new identity, that proper to the reality of Jesus as Son. The mutual indwelling formula says that the *two* become *one* without ceasing to be *two*.[11]

---

9. In John the word *kathôs* often does not simply introduce a comparison but conveys the idea of a foundation or an originating cause; see X. Léon-Dufour, "Quelques textes de portée mystique," in *Origine et Postérité de l'Évangile de Jean* (Lectio divina 143; Paris: Cerf, 1990) 261f.

10. I. de la Potterie, "Il Buon Pastore," in his *Studi di Cristologia giovannea*, 103.

11. See X. Léon-Dufour, *Lettura del Vangelo secondo Giovanni* (3 vols.; Cinisello Balsamo-Milan: Ed. Paoline, 1989, 1992, 1995) 3:210.

As we go through the gospel, we find that John uses the formula in a very consistent manner. It is used to express both the relationship between Jesus and the Father and that between Jesus and believers.[12] In both uses Jesus is the "place" in which the relationship of intimacy between the Father and believers and between believers among themselves becomes a reality; he is the mediator.

In Jesus the believer has the same relationship with the Father that the Son does, but with the difference that the believer is identified with Christ. The believer, like the Son, is "turned toward the bosom of the Father" (see 1:18).[13] Léon-Dufour describes the relationship in this way: "The disciple is transfigured from within: His new being is that of the Son. The result is the fulfillment of the plan of God, who created Adam 'in his image.' On the other hand, since love requires the existence of *two*, there is never a fusion of God and human being, nor a confusion between them."[14]

Thus united with Christ to the point of being Christ, although the difference between them remains, the believer receives the gift of sonship and is introduced into the life

---

12. The formula is not used in the fourth gospel (unlike 1 John) for the relationship between the Father and believers, nor for that of believers among themselves. John is certainly familiar with the idea of the Father dwelling in the heart of the believer (14:23), but in expressing this idea he avoids the formula of reciprocal immanence, because the relationship between the Father and the believer becomes a reality in Jesus. The same holds for the relationship among believers, which may be called a reciprocal indwelling insofar as every distance between brothers and sisters is removed in Jesus, who is the "place" in which the scattered are brought together into unity (Jn 11:52; see also Gal 3:28).

13. In this connection C. H. Dodd says in his *The Interpretation of the Fourth Gospel* (Cambridge: Cambridge University Press, 1968): "The love of God, thus released into history, brings men into the same unity of which the relation of Father and Son is the eternal archetype" (262).

14. Léon-Dufour, *Lettura*, 3:213.

of the Trinity. The believer is a "child of God" (Jn 1:12; 11:52; 1 Jn 3:1, 2, 10; 5:2).[15]

As I pointed out just above, in the allegory of the vine and the branches John several times uses the verb "remain in/dwell in."[16] It is worth our while to linger on this point for a moment. The Greek verb *menein* conveys the idea of dwelling (or staying: see 1:38) and the idea of permanence and fidelity (remaining). To a certain extent, it complements the verb "to believe." The idea, then, is to persevere in one's life in the close communion of being and love with Jesus to which the person has access through faith. It is not surprising, then, that in John 15:4 the first part of the formula shows the verb in the imperative mood: "Remain in me, and I in you."

What conditions must the believer satisfy in order to remain in Jesus and thereby in communion with the Father?

John singles out two:

• Observance of the word of Jesus (Jn 14:21ff. and 15:10; see 5:38; 8:31).

• Reception of the eucharist.

The value which the evangelist assigns to this sacrament is to be seen in John 6:53ff., and in vv. 56-57 in particular:

Whoever eats my flesh and drinks my blood
dwells in me and I in him.

---

15. The evangelist maintains the distinction even in his choice of words. In speaking of the divine sonship of the believer he uses the Greek word *teknon* ("child"), which is never used of Jesus; on the other hand, the Greek word *huios* ("son") is reserved for Jesus. This is a distinction which Paul (for example) does not make (see Cilia, *La morte di Gesù*, 56, note 47).

16. The verb occurs 40 times in the fourth gospel, 11 times in chapter 15 alone. The phrase "remain in/dwell in" with a religious meaning is characteristically Johannine (see Lazure, *Les Valeurs morales*, 31ff.)

As the Father, the living One, has sent me,
and I live thanks to the Father,
so too whoever eats me will live thanks to me.

R. Schnackenburg writes: "In this verse [56] we find for the first time in the fourth gospel an 'immanence formula,' expressing in a characteristic way the insurpassable close union between Christians and Christ. . . . In the earthly and human sphere there is no counterpart to such mutual permeation without surrender of personality."[17]

The formula of reciprocal indwelling, which is found only here in the first part of the gospel, is especially powerful. It also shows us that for the evangelist the eucharist is par excellence the sacrament which, in the present life, identifies believers with Christ and accomplishes in an ineffable way the mystery of the *two* in *one*,[18] access to which is made possible by faith and becomes a reality through knowledge and love.

3. The Believer in the Community

We would be mistaken if we were to infer from this intimate and highly personal relation between the believer and Christ that John is offering an individualistic spirituality and if we were therefore to accuse him of "soteriological individualism," that is, of proposing a private and entirely individual salvation. The Johannine conception of faith is not in fact a matter of interiority; it urges us not to a private

---

17. Schnackenburg, *The Gospel according to John*, 2:63.
18. See Léon-Dufour, *Lettura* 2:216.

call to contemplation but to love of our brothers and sisters.[19]

In the view of the evangelist there is no living of Christian life without or apart from the community.[20]

Like the other major New Testament ecclesiologies,[21] that of John brings out the Christological dimension. While faith takes the form of a complete adherence to Christ, yet the latter's role is not limited to receiving the individuals accepted by the Father (see Jn 6:44ff.; 17:6). The acceptance of individuals is part of the broader plan "to bring together into unity the scattered children of God" (11:51f.). "The Johannine Christ mediates God's life to each of those who receive and keep his word and also, in addition to this, includes them in the community of believers assigned and entrusted to him."[22]

The Johannine conception of the Church emerges especially in the allegory of the Good Shepherd and in that of the vine and the branches.

In John 10 attention is focused on the mutuality of knowledge between the shepherd and each of his sheep; this subject ends with the statement that there is a single flock around the single Shepherd. As F. M. Braun remarks, "John moves from the interior to the exterior, from union with Christ through faith to the community of those who belong

---

19. See I. de la Potterie, "La fede negli scritti giovannei," in his *Studi di Cristologia giovannea*, 299.

20. Schnackenburg, *The Gospel according to John* 3:209.

21. Compare the ecclesiology of Matthew, according to which the presence of Christ in the community is the fulfillment of the covenant, and the ecclesiology of Paul, according to which our being incorporated "into Christ" includes a being incorporated into his body, the community.

22. Schnackenburg, *The Gospel according to John*, 3:211.

to him."[23] Faith understood as a "dwelling in Christ" is the basis for establishing believers as a single flock (to keep the image used by Jesus) and not as scattered individuals. When brought together in Christ, previously scattered believers are also brought close to one another.

The allegory of the vine and the branches is no less meaningful.[24] In the Old Testament the image of the vine is often applied to Israel (Is 5:1-7; 27:2-3; and so on). In John it is an essentially collective image: Jesus and believers form a single living reality that is fed by the same sap and the same vine. Anyone on the "vine" who does not share in this life-giving circulation is cut off and then dies. Believers are alive and bear fruit only to the extent that they are inserted into the "vine." Consequently, it is only united in Christ, as a people, that they go to God.

In the allegory, John emphasizes the "dwelling in Christ, who is the vine," that is, he stresses the life-giving relationship with Jesus and with others. J. M. R. Tillard writes:

> The allegory of the vine obviously sheds light on the words "that they may be one" of chapter 17. It sheds light, above all, on the ecclesiological meaning of the commandment of fraternal love. . . . The commandment "Love one another as (*kathôs*) I have loved you" (15:12, 17) is not to be understood as an added obligation, a precept over and above the law of Christian life. No, it is that without which there would no longer be a vine, but only a bundle of barren branches

---

23. F. M. Braun,, *La foi chrétienne selon Saint Jean* (Paris: Gabalda, 1976) 64.

24. This allegory is often regarded as the Johannine equivalent of Paul's conception of the community as the body of Christ.

that have no sap. Not to love the *other* disciples means to place oneself outside the *Agapê* of the Father and the Son, in which we must *dwell* if we are to be disciples (see 15:10). If we lack love of our brothers and sisters, we separate ourselves from the vine, we cut ourselves off both from Jesus and others.[25]

Shortly before this passage, the same author has this reflection: "The relationship with Jesus is never a relationship with Jesus alone, a Jesus locked within the limits of his own personality, isolated in his transcendence. It is always in his relationship both to the Father and to those whom the gospel calls his *friends* that his disciples are united with him."

There can be no doubt: According to John, faith, being a personal encounter with Christ, does not enclose the believer in a private and solitary devotion to him; on the contrary, it even structures him in depth as a person open to others. Faith leads to action; this accounts for the close connection which the evangelist, obeying the logic of the theology of covenant, establishes between "believing," that is, "loving Jesus" and "observing/keeping the word of Jesus."[26]

---

25. See J. M. R. Tillard, *Chair de l'Église, chair du Christ* (Cogitatio Fidei 168; Paris: Cerf, 1992) 28.

26. "Whoever receives my commandments and keeps them loves me. . . . Whoever loves me will keep my word" (14:21, 23). The connection between loving Jesus and keeping the commandments is in continuity with the theology of the Sinai covenant. To love Yahweh—which is the fundamental commandment—means living in communion with him and accepting without reservation his will that finds expression in the particular commandments. In the structure of the covenant there is a close bond between the relationship with God and the observance of the conditions for life in community; in other words, an authentic relationship with Yahweh within the covenant can be attained only through a right moral and social behavior. The connection between loving God and loving one's neighbor makes necessary a spirituality of communion.

4. Believing and Keeping the Word

Faith, then, does not isolate the believer in a solitary relationship with Christ and with God. In the fourth gospel, the verb "believe" alternates with other expressions, such as "love Jesus" and "observe/keep his commandments/the word." The fact that "believe" means both "cleaving to Jesus" and "keeping his word" shows the close connection between faith and a concrete behavior.[27] The evangelist states the connection in a few words in 14:15: "If you love me, you will keep my commandments."

The love which Jesus requires of his followers is not so much a sentiment; rather, as in the Septuagint, it is a complete adherence to him that finds expression precisely in living a life of fidelity to his demands.[28] That is the definition of a believer.

Faith, then, urges in two closely connected directions: toward entrance into a very close relationship with Christ and toward entrance into the relational reality of his being as Son. But this twofold relationship is lived out not by withdrawing into private devotion but by keeping his commandments.[29]

It is a fact that the evangelist never gives in detail the precise content of these "commandments." It is important, however, to note the passage from the plural to the singular in 15:10-12:

---

27. See R. Bultmann, "Pisteuô," *Theological Dictionary of the New Testament* 6:227-28.

28. See C. Spicq, *Agapè dans le Nouveau Testament* 3 (Paris: Gabalda, 1969) 182.

29. *Têrein tas entolas/ton logon* is a Johannine expression (8:51; 14:23f.; 15:10, 20; 1 Jn 2:3-5; 3:22, 24; 5:3) that has its place in Jewish religious culture (sapiential writings: Prv 3:1, 21; Tb 14:9; etc.; and Qumran: *1 QS* 5:8-9, 20-22; etc.). See Spicq, *Agapè* 3:182, note 3.

10a. If you keep my commandments,
you will remain in my love. . . .
12. This is my commandment:
that you love one another
as I have loved you.

When John speaks of "commandments" in the plural, he is always and in every case referring to a concrete activity,[30] not to velleities or good intentions of doing the divine will. This is clear from 1 John 3:17-18:

If a man has the riches of this world but, seeing his brother in need, closes his heart to him, how does the love of God dwell in him? Little children, let us love not in words or with the tongue, but in deeds and in truth.

The various commandments are all directed to the commandment par excellence, which is the commandment of mutual love. The activity of the believer in keeping the various commandments receives its direction and finality from mutual love. Such behavior has essentially a single goal: the life of unity in the community. Given this perspective, there is no need to list the various commandments; each of these derives its meaning and content from the way in which the fundamental commandment is put into practice in each situation.

"Believing" calls for a very concrete "doing," but not in

30. The plural "commandments" expresses the will of the Father or of the Son in its entirety. John is not referring to a catalogue of laws or precepts; his emphasis is more on the complete revelation of the divine will than on a numerical plurality. See Lazure, *Les Valeurs morales*, 126f.

the Pauline sense of "doing works." Even though the evangelist uses the formula "keep the commandments" (14:15, 21; 15:10),[31] he gives the expression a meaning much deeper than that of a simple observance of the precepts of the Torah. This is suggested by other formulations, such as "remain in the word" (8:31), "have the word abiding in oneself" (15:7), and "have a place in oneself for the word" (8:37).[32]

A life-giving relationship is established between the word and the believer. To abide in the word means "not only to hear it but to assimilate it so as to derive life from it and make it the norm and inspiration of one's life."[33]

The word, for its part, makes its way into believers; the result is a process of interiorization, which is effected by the Holy Spirit (14:26; 16:13f.) and increasingly transforms believers into those-who-love (15:9-10). The word becomes in them a source of light and strength for all of their concrete activity in the community.[34] Consequently, it also increasingly conforms them to the filial life of Jesus.

Everything starts with the revealed word, which, if accepted, unfolds in the depths of believers its mys-

---

31. The corresponding Greek verb *têrein* means both "keep/preserve" and "observe/practice."

32. The terms "commandments" and "word" are not completely interchangeable. When John shifts from "commandments" in the plural to "word" in the singular, we must think that he is making a qualitative leap. Van den Bussche, *Jean* (Paris: Desclée de Brouwer, 1967): "We would impoverish the meaning of 'word' if we were to think of it simply as the word uttered by Jesus, for it expresses the whole of revelation, which is Jesus himself." See also F. M. Braun, *Jean le Théologien* 3/1 (Paris: Gabalda, 1972) 115f.

33. U. Mannucci, *Giovanni, Vangelo narrante* (Bologna: EDB, 1993) 127.

34. de la Potterie, "La fede" (note 19, above) 298.

terious but nonetheless experienced energies. In addition to enlightening the mind through a supernatural understanding of the Christian mystery (1 Jn 4:2), these energies give rise to specific sentiments, those of God, which create a kind of connaturality with things divine (1 Jn 4:6b), so that believers are attracted by them (1 Jn 4:9b) and are spurred on to act in accordance with their demands. (1 Jn 1:7c)[35]

John saves the faithful from dream-woven pious illusions of a direct vision of the godhead that is accompanied by intense feelings and profound fervor. To remain in the love of Jesus and find in him an intimate relationship with the Father requires the concrete observance of commandments directed at living in love of one's brothers and sisters. This is the sure way to an authentic encounter with God and to the experience of the fullness of joy that this encounter brings with it (see 15:11).[36]

---

35. Dalbesio, *Quello che abbiamo* (note 4, above) 136.

36. On this point see the reflections of J. Huby, *Le discours de Jésus après la Cène* (Paris, 1942) 79f.

Chapter 3

The Human Response: Love

Introduction

We have seen that for John faith and love are inseparable. "Faith leads the person into the dynamism of love; in John's eyes, then, faith in Jesus and love form so close-knit a whole that for him faith is real only if the believer becomes one-who-loves."[1]

In the first part of the gospel (chapters 1–12) John presents the public life of Jesus as a confrontation between Jesus and the world of humanity, whose direct representatives are the Jews. The verb "believe," understood as a call to accept the word of the Revealer, predominates.

In the second part (chapters 13–17), Jesus is with his disciples, and his words have the Last Supper as their setting. From chapter 13 on, he is alone with his followers; he no longer debates with "those outside" (*hoi exô*). What is presented in the first part as sign and promise, as revelation and call, is now fulfilled in the disciples gathered around Jesus. The disciples are those who have accepted the

1. U. Mannucci, *Giovanni, Vangelo narrante* (Bologna: EDB, 1993) 325.

word of Jesus and believe; in short, they represent the Christian community. Jesus speaks to them of problems and situations that directly affect them; in other words, he speaks of the life of the post-Easter Church, which is marked by the absence of Jesus.

True enough, the last part of the gospel contains the account of the passion and the appearances of the risen Lord. In this respect, John is following the tradition. But it can be said, from another point of view, that the ideal conclusion of the gospel consists of the section containing the farewell discourse. The Jesus who addresses the disciples in chapters 13–17 is already one who speaks when the "hour" has been accomplished, that is, one in full possession of the saving power acquired on the cross. Therefore, even though the farewell discourse comes before the account of the passion-glorification of Jesus, it actually presupposes this: Jesus is already speaking to the entire Church, which is represented by the disciples, and the perspective is postpaschal. It is in these chapters that the evangelist deals directly with the mystery, identity, and problems of the Christian community.

The themes change from those of the first part, and simple statistics on the use of words are already revealing. Thus the expression "give life," which occurs 50 times in the first part, occurs only 6 times in the second; the word "light" occurs 32 times in the first part but not at all in the second. On the other hand, "to love/love," which occur only 6 times in the first part, occur 31 times in the second; conversely, the verb "believe" occurs 76 times in the first part, but only 22 times in chapters 13–21.

The statistics correspond to the overall approach taken in the gospel: from faith to fraternal love as expression of love for Jesus. The call to faith that runs through the entire first part is concretized in the communion of the disciples around Jesus, which in turn prefigures the mutual indwelling of the risen Jesus and believers in the post-Easter Church.

To speak of love, then, is to come to the core of the Johannine discourse on faith and on observance of the demands of Jesus.

In the chapters of the farewell discourse we expect to find the ethical teaching of the fourth gospel. And yet John does not take up concrete questions of morality and religious life, such as riches, divorce, and so on. He focuses his attention on the basic Christian attitude: to keep the word of Jesus, to remain in Jesus, to love one's brothers and sisters. At times, the tone is exhortatory, but the evangelist does not stay on the parenetic level, since in his view there is a deeper level even to ethical teaching: the level of revelation. He is speaking of the deeper identity of the community. When John exhorts believers to live their faith, his purpose is not so much to urge them to improve their behavior as it is to have them become aware of their identity, of the divine mystery that gives them their being. John sets forth a theological ethics.

1. *Love in the Fourth Gospel*

Let us turn our attention now to the subject of love, which is dominant in the second part of the gospel.

Dodd is right in saying that even though the theme of faith in Jesus as bringer of light and life is for practical purposes absent from the second part of the gospel, the evangelist does not intend to replace it with the concept of

love. He intends only to stress the point that the reality of
life and light is fully given in the reality of *agapê*. It is in the
life of *agapê* that believers know God and share in his life.[2]

In John's view, *agapê* is God's life that has been communicated to believers.

Immediately following upon the allegory of the vine and
the branches, Jesus says:

> As the Father has loved me,
> so I have loved you;
> remain in my love.
> If you keep my commandments,
> you will remain in my love,
> as I have kept my Father's commandment
> and remain in his love.
> (15:9-10)

The verses are connected with the allegory of the vine and
the branches, being to some extent an explanation and deeper
understanding of it. The one sap flows from the vine to
branches and unites them; the reality that unites Jesus and
his disciples is nothing other than the eternal love of the
Father for the Son, a love which the Son has given to his
followers and which he wants to see circulating among them.

Since it is of divine origin, the *agapê* that inspires love of
one's brothers and sisters has the characteristics of the love
that Jesus revealed in his life and, above all, in his death. It
is a love that leads to the giving of the lover's life: "No one
has a greater love than this: to give his life for his friends"

---

2. C. H. Dodd, *The Interpretation of the Fourth Gospel* (Cambridge: Cambridge
University Press, 1953) 398.

(15:13; see 1 Jn 3:16f.). But in giving their life for a brother or a sister, believers live the life and experience the love of the Father and of Jesus (14:21, 23; 16:27).

In his first Letter, John makes it clear that the love coming from God and lived out among the brethren does not simply lead to moral behavior. Rather it is something ontic, something of being, for in this love there is a passage from existence "in death" to existence "in life" (5:24; 1 Jn 3:14f.).[3]

Agapê goes beyond human love but does not negate it; quite the contrary. But it is opposed to the love characteristic of the "world," that is, human beings closed to revelation. Proof of the divine origin of fraternal love is given by the reaction of withdrawal and hostility which this love can arouse and which can treat believers as aliens (15:18f.), precisely because the love between brothers and sisters seems like an alien body in the world (17:14).[4]

The love of God that has been revealed and communicated by Jesus becomes, then, a source of the love lived out in the community, but it also makes its demands: The observance of the commandment par excellence (15:17) is the condition for remaining in the love of Christ and, consequently, for sharing, through a life of fraternal communion, in that love with which the Father has always loved the Son. "This is how it is: The Father loves the Son, the Son loves his followers, the disciples love one another. Love is the root, the trunk, and the fruit of this life that has its roots in eternity and extends its branches throughout the entire world."[5]

---

3. See the reflections of H. Schlier, "Die Bruderliebe nach dem Evangelium und den Briefen des Johannes," in *Mélanges bibliques en hommage au R. P. Béda B. Rigaux* (Gembloux: Duculot, 1969) 244.

4. Ibid., 245.

5. Spicq, *Agapè* 3:170.

There is certainly no room for an individualistic spirituality in a world in which the Father's plan comes to fruition when the same divine life circulates among the divine persons and the community of believers to which all are called, so that the divine persons and the community become one (amid the distinction between them). That kind of spirituality erects a barrier against the *agapê* that originates in the Father and is communicated by Jesus to those who receive him, so that it may circulate among human beings with unity as the goal.

2. Mutual Love: 13:34-35

John never explicitly mentions the love of neighbor or of enemies that was so characteristic of the teaching of Jesus. This is not due to forgetfulness nor does it deserve to be reproached as sectarianism. John's attention is focused essentially on the life of the Christian community, as is demonstrated by the entire setting of the farewell discourse (chapters 13–17).

The evangelist applies the teaching of Jesus on love of neighbor to the life of the community and therefore speaks of mutual love. In so doing, he reveals the goal of love of neighbor: This love seeks to become a communion in love; it is directed toward a neighbor who becomes a brother or sister.[6] The *agapê* that comes from God reaches its high

---

6. St. Augustine, *Homilies on the First Letter of John*: "Love all human beings, even your enemies, not because they are your brothers and sisters but in order that they may become such; and be always on fire with brotherly love, both for the one who is already your brother and for your enemy, in order that by loving him he may become a brother."

point in reciprocity and therefore tends to the life of unity
as to its end: "If we love one another, God remains in us,
and his love is made perfect in us" (1 Jn 4:12bc).

Faith makes but one other fundamental demand: It calls
for the mutual love that sums up the "doing" of believers
in relation to their brothers and sisters, a "doing" that is
ordered to the life of unity:

> I give you a new commandment:
> love one another!
> Yes, love one another
> with the love with which I have loved you.
> By this shall everyone know that you are my disciples:
> if you have love for one another.
> (Jn 13:34-35)

These two verses have no direct connection with the
context in which they are placed, for they interrupt the
discussion of Jesus' departure (see vv. 33 and 36). But they
have been inserted intentionally, for they are meant to
answer the problem that is created by the departure of Jesus
and that marks the situation of the post-Easter Church.[7]

Why does Jesus describe as "new" the commandment

---

7. These two verses are very close in vocabulary, style, and content to the
first Letter of John, and there may be a literary dependence:
—"new" commandment: The phrase occurs only in John 13:32 and in
1 John 2:7-8; 2 John 5;
—"little children": Jn 13:13 and 1 Jn 2:1, 12, 28; 3:7, 18; 4:4; 5:21;
—"in this" + verb "to know": Jn 13:35; 1 Jn 2:3, 5; 3:16, 19, 24; 4:2,
13; 5:2.
There is also a kinship with the prayer for unity in 17:21-23:
—the construction of the phrases using "in order to" and "as" (*kathôs*);
—the universal perspective: "all" in 13:35; the "world" (in a positive
sense) in 17:23.

that must characterize the life of his disciples? There is certainly an allusion to the covenant of Yahweh with Israel, which receives its definitive fulfillment. The commandment is however "new," essentially because the love itself is new in nature: It is the filial love of Jesus, which is the origin and foundation of a new dispensation of relations that establish an entirely new human family.

The usual translation, "Love one another as I have loved you," is too weak, because it conveys the idea that Jesus is simply a model to be imitated. The words should rather be translated: "Love one another with the love with which I have loved you," in order to retain the meaning of the adverb *kathôs*.[8] If the adverb is read as simply pointing to a parallel, "we end up turning Jesus into a person of the past, from whom we have inherited instructions to be applied by later individuals, so that the action of the disciples comes in temporal succession to that of Jesus and is juxtaposed with it."[9] Now, rather, it is Christ himself and his filial love that become present in the mutual love of the disciples: "His love passes into them when they love the brethren and are loved by them in return."[10]

When Jesus gives the commandment of mutual love as his response to the problem caused by his departure, he inaugurates his permanent presence among his followers. The relationship which he has had with his disciples during his earthly life and which was a reflection of his oneness with the Father, must now be changed after his departure into a fraternal love in the community.

---

8. See X. Léon-Dufour, *Lettura del Vangelo secondo Giovanni* (Cinisello Balsamo-Milan: Ed. Paoline, 1989-95) 3:106f.

9. Ibid., 107.

10. Ibid.

Several characteristics of mutual love become intelligible in light of this meaning of "new":
• If this mutual love is a reflection of the love of Jesus (which in turn is a revelation of his filial relationship with and love of the Father), then

> it is understandable that it cannot be reduced to a few well-defined precepts imposed from outside, but must, like life itself, be capable of countless, undefined, universal applications. It is up to each Christian to accept a personal responsibility and identify at each moment the way in which to ensure that the dynamism of the divine *agapê* transforms all the concrete actions of life.[11]

• Love between believers follows the same standard as Christ's love did: the standard of the gift of life. But, as Lazure warns: "It is not enough to wait for an occasion for laying down our life for those whom we love (15:13); on the contrary, we must, like him [Jesus], place ourselves at the humble service of the brothers and sisters at each moment of our life."[12] In other words, "to give one's life" is an abiding mark of Christian love.

Love shows itself to have a further mark. Léon-Dufour writes:

> In 13:34 the love of Jesus is unqualified and therefore more comprehensive. Its supreme expression was

---

11. N. Lazure, *Les Valeurs morales de la Théologie johannique* (Paris: Gabalda, 1965) 231.
12. Ibid.

indeed the cross (see 13:1), but the cross represented a movement inherent in the being of the Son, as Jesus will make clear in 15:9: "With the love with which the Father has loved me, so have I loved you." Consequently, while the fraternal love of believers can demand a supreme gift, it is first of all a state, namely, their way of life in union with the Son.[13]

In mutual love believers embody the filial reality of Christ in the bosom of the Father.

• The love to be lived in community "is a gift received, rather than a moral requirement; it is the sign that the life of believers is in continuity with the divine communion in which they share."[14]

It is because of this that mutual love has the "revelatory" character and function that is presupposed in verse 35. The mutual love that makes the love of Jesus present makes known his identity as Son, his relationship with the Father, and therefore the love of the Father himself, who has sent his Only-Begotten and makes himself accessible to humanity.

As a result, the community that is united by mutual love continues to be a sign for the world, just as Jesus was by the way he acted; a sign that can elicit either faith or hatred,

---

13. Léon-Dufour, *Lettura*, 3:107. The love of the Son is not purely and simply that of the pre-existent Logos who is eternally turned toward the bosom of the Father; it is that same love as lived out now by Jesus on earth and reaching its high point on the cross. The eternal love of the Son is no longer separable from the love of Jesus lifted up. See T. Onuki, *Gemeinde und Welt im Johannesevangelium* (WMANT 56; Neukirchen: Neukirchener Verlag, 1984) 177f.: The way to the Father is the crucified Jesus, just as the crucified Jesus is the way travelled by the divine *agapê* for humanity.

14. Léon-Dufour, *Lettura*, 3:109.

acceptance or rejection. "In leaving Christians the commandment to love one another as he has loved us, Christ gives them the responsibility of continuing in the world that manifestation of divine *agapê* that he began."[15]
If love, due to its divine origin, is meant to spread throughout the world, then any tendency to individualism or to a closing in of the community on itself (there is such a thing as a collective individualism!) becomes unthinkable. "If fraternal love is the primary and effective sign that overcomes the unbelief of the outside world, then it cannot at the same time be the means by which the community practices a sectarian isolation."[16]
It is possible to go even further:

> Christians recognize one another by a single sign, that of mutual love. If this love is lacking, the presence of Christ in our world through his Church can no longer be seen. The practice of *agapê*, therefore, cannot be approached from a purely individual vantage point that engages only the relations of each individual person with God. On the contrary, it has a community dimension; the lack of it in a disciple, who thereby veils the presence of Christ from the eyes of others, casts discredit on the Church of which the disciple claims to be a member.[17]

15. Lazure, *Les Valeurs morales*, 230.
16. Mannucci, *Giovanni* (note 1, above) 326.
17. Lazure, *Les Valeurs morales*, 231.

3. Johannine Mysticism

Is it possible to describe as "mystical" the experience of faith that John sets before his readers?

At the end of the Prologue to his gospel, John says: "No one has ever seen God" (1:18a).

By placing faith in Jesus and the gift of *agapê* to be lived out among the brethren at the basis of Christian life, the evangelist makes known the possibility of a union with God that has no parallel and is expressed in language familiar to the mystics: contemplation, communion with God, reciprocal indwelling, knowledge, and so on. We read in C. H. Dodd:

> He [John] makes use of the strongest expressions for union with God that contemporary religious language provided, in order to assure his readers that he does seriously mean what he says: that through faith in Christ we may enter into a personal community of life with the eternal God, which has the character of *agapê*, which is essentially supernatural and not of this world, and yet plants its feet firmly in this world, not only because real *agapê* cannot but express itself in practical conduct, but also because the crucial act of *agapê* was actually performed in history, on an April day about A.D. 30, at a supper-table in Jerusalem, in a garden across the Kidron valley, in the headquarters of Pontius Pilate, and on a Roman cross at Golgotha. So concrete, so actual, is the nature of the divine *agapê*; yet nonetheless for that, by entering into the relation of *agapê* thus opened up for men, we may dwell in God and He in us.

Dodd ends by saying: "Whether this should be called 'mysticism' I do not know."[18]

It is enough here that we agree on the meaning of the term "mysticism." In a formulation that captures the essence and is at the same time simple, John gives the key to the goal of all mysticism, namely, union with God: "No one has ever seen God. If we love one another, God remains in us and his love is perfect in us" (1 Jn 4:12).

Through faith a human being is united to Jesus, who alone is the revealer of God. But oneness with Jesus and thereby with the Father is not obtained through ecstasy and a flight from other persons, but through a mutual love that is an expression of love of God and for God. By loving its brothers and sisters the soul has no need to renounce the body in order to set out on a difficult climb to heights inaccessible to ordinary mortals. Rather, it is God himself who comes down and makes his dwelling in the believer: "The desired communion with God—with the Father and his Son Jesus—can be achieved and brought to completion only when, through mutual love, we remain in God's love."[19]

> "Whoever has my commandments and keeps them
> loves me;
> and whoever loves me will be loved by my Father,
> and I too will love him and show myself to him."
> Judas (not the Iscariot) says to him:
> "Lord, how is it that you are to show yourself to us

---

18. Dodd, *Interpretation*, 199-200.
19. R. Schnackenburg, *Die sittliche Botschaft des Neuen Testamentes* (2 vols.; Freiburg i. B.: Herder, 1988) 2:176.

and not to the world?"
Jesus answered him and said to him:
"Whoever loves me will keep my word,
and my Father will love him,
and we will come to him
and make a dwelling with him."
(Jn 14:21-23)

Verse 21 is a repetition in positive terms of verse 15, in which a conditional statement was made: "If you love me, you will keep my commandments." Readers now know that their love for the Lord becomes real in the observance of his word, that is, by living according to the example which Jesus himself gave when he washed the feet of his disciples and gave his life for his followers. This way of acting brings believers into the relationship of Jesus with the Father, so that, like the Son, they too are the object of the Father's love.

Jesus is not a figure of the past who has left to posterity a more or less relevant teaching known as Christianity. Today, as in his day, it is necessary to believe in him and develop a living, personal relationship with him in order to enter into communion with God. He is *the* Revealer.[20]

In the verse we have just examined, first place is given to the Father's love; secondly, it is said that Jesus too will love and show himself to the believer. From this it is clear that as mediator, Jesus puts the believer, who has become one with him, in direct communion with the Father. But once the believer is placed in the bosom of the Father, in the Father's inmost being, he also meets Jesus as a distinct Thou, while experiencing his love in an increasing degree.

---

20. J. Blank, *Das Evangelium nach Johannes* (Düsseldorf: Patmos, 1981) 3:116f.

Judas' interruption—a literary device the evangelist habitually uses—leads to a more specific statement: Jesus is not speaking of his glorious parousia at the end of time, when he will be manifested to all human beings, but of a presence of God that is henceforth possible in the heart of the believer and in the midst of the community.

Verse 23 ends with a phrase, "we will . . . make a dwelling with him," that evokes the expected dwelling of God with his people, which was prefigured by the Jerusalem temple and then proclaimed by the prophets as a hope for the future: "I am coming to dwell in the midst of you" (Zec 2:14). And this is how he whom "neither the heavens nor the heavens of the heavens can contain" is coming to make his dwelling henceforth and for ever within the believer and in the midst of the community.

When they are united to Jesus, who is par excellence the holy place of the divine presence, believers in their turn can, through mutual love, become the dwelling of the divine persons and a revelation of divine love to all of humanity.

At the beginning of the chapter Jesus had promised his disciples that "in my Father's house there are many places. . . . I am going to prepare a place for you" (14:2). Without negating or renouncing this promise, the evangelist changes his perspective: "The movement, sketched in 14:2-3, of the disciples to the Father under the guidance of Jesus is reversed: It is the Father who comes to the faithful disciple. . . . The quest for the Father, which is the essential theme of the discourse right from its beginning (13:33), is completed by the Father himself."[21]

---

21. Léon-Dufour, *Lettura* 3:163.

The question is sometimes asked whether John is setting forth a morality or a mysticism, but there is no basis for such an alternative. Since communion with the Father and the Son is the wellspring of the believer's activity, ethical behavior (that is, love of the brethren) and mysticism (that is, union with God) are inseparable from one another.

> There has often been talk of a Johannine *mysticism of God*. The commandment of love, however, separates such a mysticism from any religious outlook current at that time and surfacing again today: the religiosity that aspires to a communion with God that is pantheistic or ecstatic or magical or gnostic, or anything else. Love of the brethren decides in practice whether we are "from the truth" (1 Jn 3:19). It is the sure sign of our union with God. John the *mystic* is a concrete, Christian realist.[22]

John does not address his work to any kind of elite who live in the seclusion of a monastery, but to all believers who live their daily lives in the midst of other people. They can share in the life of the Trinity even now, but only if through mutual love they remain in the *agapê* of God.

---

22. Schnackenburg, *Die sittliche Botschaft* 2:176. See 1 Jn 2:10; 3:14, 17; 4:12, 16.

Chapter 4

The Prayer for Unity: John 17:20-23

On the one hand, the fourth gospel presents the life and activity of Jesus as a revelation of God. The coming of Christ and the unveiling of the filial mystery of his person are intended to bring humanity to a knowledge of God in his inmost life. On the other hand, John gives us the response of human beings who open themselves to faith and to a life that culminates in mutual love. The revelation of God as Trinity has the unity of believers as its salvific purpose.

In the prayer for unity, these two aspects are brought together and combined at a new level: The "we" of the community has its completion in the "we" of God. Trinity of God open to humanity, the unity of believers in God: The love of God is now complete, that is, it reaches its goal.

But John carefully distinguishes between mutual love and unity. In the farewell discourse up to chapter 17, he speaks only of mutual love (13:34f.; 15:12, 17); this is a command of Jesus and an obligation, even though *agapê* is divine in origin. Being *one* is instead something asked of God for the disciples: Unity is a divine gift. Unlike mutual love, unity is not within the scope of exhortation. It transcends the realm of ethics, even while remaining fundamentally connected with ethics, since the real unity of human beings does not exist apart from their manifestation of mutual love.

For John, then, unity is not to be confused with good team-work or with the harmony that reigns among members of an association, although, of course, it does not exclude these things. Unity does not arise from the combined efforts of believers nor is it based on philosophical principles, as, for example, on the nature shared by all human beings. Unity is essentially a characteristic of God: It is his way of being a communion. From the viewpoint of human beings, therefore, unity is a gift given to us in Christ; it is the gift of being one in Christ and the gift of the law that governs the movement of the interior life of the divine persons. Unity becomes a reality through living—in God and in the manner of God—according to the law of God's being as communion.

In the prayer for unity—which is at the same time a revelatory prayer and discourse—John urges the Church to become aware of the trinitarian law that is at the basis of fraternal relationships. He wants to see realized in the concrete life of the community the kind of relationship that exists among the divine persons. This is possible because among believers who love one another there circulates the very love with which the Father loves the Son. One and the same love that unites Father and Son and makes them be one also unites believers among themselves and introduces them into the dynamism of the divine life. Between speaker and listener, between giver and receiver there arises the same kind of relationship that marks the communion of the Father and the Son.

All this is summed up in the central part of the prayer:

[20] I pray not only for them
but for those who
through their word will believe
in me,
[21] so that they all may be one
as you, Father,
in me and I in you,
so that they too may be
one in us,
so that the world may believe
that you have sent me.

[22] I have given them the glory

which you have given me,

so that they may be one
as we are one,
I in them and you in me,
so that they may be perfect
in unity,
so that the world may realize
that you have sent me
and have loved them
as you have loved me.

The statement about being one is developed in two parallel sentences that complement one another. But first, in verse 20, the evangelist must remind his readers that the prayer is not limited to the historical disciples of Jesus but embraces all who believe in him, all future generations. The prayer of Jesus is offered for believers of all times and all places.

It is now possible, in the light of Johannine theology, to understand the content of the prayer: "being *one*" is characteristic of the relationship between the Father and Jesus, as expressed in the formula of reciprocal indwelling (v. 21); it must also be a characteristic of relationships in the community. This is possible, as verse 22 explains, through the mediation of Christ ("I in them and you in me"). In Jesus, believers experience the fatherhood of God and find a place in God himself ("in us"): In God they live out the reality of the Son to whom the Father communicates everything (5:20).

It is not a matter, then, of a simple union of a moral kind, but of a unity at the level of being, a unity that has as its model and permanent source (this is the force of the adverb *kathôs*) the oneness of the Father and the Son. Nor is it any longer a matter of a merely figurative or external, metaphorical fatherhood of God, as in the Old Testament, but of the fatherhood that relates from eternity to the only-begotten Son.

In John's view, there is no true unity except that of the Father and the Son. Apart from it, human beings are incapable of true unity and are scattered (see 11:52).

When Jesus prays that "all may be one," he is not referring to the ecumenical problem. At least in the gospel, John does not seem to address individual believers or even a divided community. On the contrary, he is addressing a united community and explaining to its members the mystery of their communion; the unity of which he speaks is that which shapes the Christian community on the model of the life of the Trinity.

In essence, the evangelist is showing the Church its own identity. In the process, the revelatory character of mutual love emerges; this love manifests unity and is, so to speak, the sacrament of the relational life of the divine persons. The unity of believers constitutes the true identity of the Christian community and can therefore show the world in a trustworthy manner what God is in his inmost being; consequently, it can also show humanity where the fullness of its being is to be found.

Even before verse 20-22 John had, in a sentence rich in content, referred to the unity of believers: "Holy Father, keep in your name those you have given me, so that they may be one as we are one" (17:11b). Jesus here prays that the disciples, while remaining in the world, may receive the power to remain in the Name, that is, in the person of the Father, the temple of the divine presence.

This Name has been given to the Son and constitutes his vital relationship with the Father, since by giving his Name to the Son the Father gives his whole self. Consequently, when Jesus asks that the disciples be kept in the Name given to them by the Father, he is asking that they be brought into that temple which is the very communion of the divine persons. Having received sonship, they are made able to share in the relationship of the Son with the Father.

When the disciples are thus kept in the Name, it becomes possible for them to be united with one another. What the divine persons are, each for the other, is now true also of the disciples, who have received a new manner of being. Having been introduced as sons and daughters into the living dialogue of the divine persons, believers can live their fraternal relationships according to the model and quality of the relationship between the Father and the Son.

In verse 22, the glory which Jesus communicates to his disciples, and which is required for their oneness to become a reality, corresponds to "your Name which you have given me" (v. 11). This glory is the mystery of his sonship, the splendor of his oneness with the Father; in it is manifested the total gift which the Father makes of himself. It becomes in turn a revelation of the love with which the Father loves the Son, a love now received by believers (see v. 23c).

The gift of glory implies that believers recognize Jesus in the luminous reality of his person and are introduced into his filial relationship or, in other words, into the divine unity. This is the indispensable condition for making real in them the oneness that has the divine persons for its model. One and the same love that unites Father and Son and constitutes their being as communion, also unites believers among themselves and introduces them into the life of the Trinity.

It follows from this that mutual love lived out in community becomes itself a revelation of the divine *agapê* that has opened itself to humanity.

The unity in question is by its nature a transcendent reality because it is a sharing in the divine unity.[1] It becomes visible, nonetheless, in the concreteness of mutual love and can therefore be seen from outside.

It is not surprising, then, that to his thoughts on unity the evangelist adds the idea of mission: "so that the world may believe."

John already broaches the theme of mission in verse 18: "As you have sent me into the world, so I send them into the world."

This theme is given a place within the discussion of the sanctification of the disciples: "Sanctify them in the truth." "Sanctification" is not to be understood as a kind of ritual consecration for a mission. The sanctification of the disciples means that they belong to the Father. Jesus prays that the Father would raise them up close to himself; that he would give them a place in the divine space of his fatherhood, where they can live out their new filial life, just as Jesus here on earth has sanctified himself by living out in the midst of humanity his reality as Son.[2]

---

1. See U. Vanni, *Il Vangelo secondo Giovanni. Passi scelti* (Rome: Gregorian University, 1989) 167.

2. On the theme of sanctification see I. de la Potterie, *La Vérité dans saint Jean* (Rome: Biblical Institute Press, 1977) 706-87; see also G. Rossé, *L'ultima preghiera di Gesù* (Rome: Città Nuova, 1988) 117ff.

The sanctification of the disciples is the more important goal; mission becomes possible as a consequence of their sanctification. The same is true of the petition: "I pray . . . so that they may be one . . . so that the world may believe." The important thing is being one: Unity is the primary aim of the prayer, because unity is the deeper reality of believers being in communion. The unity of believers is seen as an indispensable condition for the conversion of the world.

John is consistent: first, sanctification and unity; then, mission. We find the same logic at work again in the allegory of the vine and the branches (Jn 15): "bearing fruit" is linked to the need of "abiding in the love of Jesus."

What may be called the "principle of interiorization" is fundamental in John. By "interiorization" I mean the movement into the divine space that is the bosom of the Father, the place where Jesus himself lives his filial relationship.

The life of the disciples consists, at one and the same time, of interiority and sending. "The disciples when sent do not leave the Father. Their remaining in the Father and in the Son is at the very heart of their mission" (A. Jaubert).

This movement of interiorization, then, does not by any means signify a flight into the spiritual realm, a withdrawal into their own inner selves. On the contrary, when the life of believers is given its place in the interior temple of the Father's bosom, it becomes relation, communion, surrender of self, an openness to the trinitarian dimension, and a participation in the trinitarian dynamism. The disciples are therefore sent into the world just as the only-begotten Son was sent.[3] In their mutual love the disciples make visible the divine reality within which they live, and they reveal the divine Love to the world to which they are sent. By living in fraternal love, which is the sign of unity, the community continues the work of Jesus in the world of human beings. By its mutual love the united community continues down the centuries the revelatory role that had first been that of Jesus. This kind of inter-personal relationship can arouse faith and bring the world to see in the proclamation of Jesus his profound truth as the one sent by God and therefore his oneness with the Father, which reveals God's love for humanity, a love made present in the community of believers.

In John's understanding of the matter it is not possible to separate the sending into the world from the very life of the community. The mission of the disciples is rooted in

---

3. Here are the fine reflections of I. de la Potterie on "truth" in John: truth is not abstract speculation about a concept, but "it is the revelation of Jesus Christ that has been interiorized by the Spirit and has become the interior principle of the believer's new life. . . . This action of the truth in the life of Christians occurs in two complementary movements: *ab extra ad intra* [from without to within] and *ab intra ad extra* [from within to without]. A first movement is that of the increasing interiorization of the truth: The truth of Jesus is to be ever increasingly assimilated by believers so that they can make real their communion with God. This law of interiorization does not mean that in order to live in the truth Christians must take flight into a spiritual realm. On the contrary: At the ṣame time as the movement to the interior they undertake a movement in the opposite direction, a thrust outward toward the brethren: The truth is the revelation of love. When received by faith, the truth becomes the new law of Christians, the dynamism at work deep in their being. It is for them 'living water,' a spring of water that leaps up into eternity (Jn 4:10-14). It is a seed (1 Jn 3:9) that produces in them the fruits of Christian life, the chief of which is fraternal love (Jn 15:8-9). Radical communion with Jesus-Truth, far from isolating believers, becomes for them a source of charity and authentic communion with the brethren. This is the paradox of the life of faith: 'the journey of the soul toward what is most interior is an exodus' (P. Agaësse)" (*La Vérité dans saint Jean*, 1014).

their identity, and the Church is on mission to the extent that it lives in accordance with its own identity. In its "being one," the community spreads beyond itself the divine mystery that dwells in it. By its unity it is a sign of the love of the Father, who sent the Son into the world to save it and bring it into intimacy with the divinity.

It needs no saying that a spirituality of communion, based on mutual love, is utterly indispensable both for the identity of the community and for its mission to humanity.

John describes the mission of the Church not as a proclamation, as the announcement of the good news (these elements are in fact implicit), but as a revelation: The mission is fruitful to the extent that the life of believers renders visible the communion of the Father and the Son and their love for humankind. This love has its goal in the Christian community, namely, communion with the Father and with the one whom he sent (1 Jn 1:3).

John goes beyond the traditional definition of mission, when this is seen as the preaching of the kerygma by evangelizers. He sees believers as themselves in a state of mission by reason of their being one.

The community that opens up to others must make visible the divine reality it bears within itself. This means the necessity of "dwelling in the divine communion" if the mission is to be fruitful. From this we understand, too, the importance which the evangelist assigns to the movement of interiorization of Christians toward God.

Only by living in unity do the disciples continue to be in the world what Jesus was in his relation to the world according to the fourth gospel. They carry on the mission of Christ the Revealer after his departure from this world.

When faced with the community that lives in unity, the world of human beings will continue to be divided into two camps: those who believe and enter into a communion with the disciples ("and our communion is with the Father and with his Son, Jesus Christ": 1 Jn 1:3), and those who persecute and reject the Church ("If they have persecuted me, they will persecute you": Jn 15:20).

This means that the confrontation between the one sent by God and humanity will continue with the Church as its intermediary. It is a confrontation of light with darkness, of truth with lies, a confrontation that will last as long as the world of human beings lasts.

John never proclaimed a utopia in which all human beings will be united within earthly history. He says only that throughout history the unity of believers will arouse either faith or hatred, just as the activity and teaching of the incarnate Son aroused either faith or hatred.

Chapter 5

The Spirituality of Communion in the First Letter of John

I have thus far focused attention exclusively on the gospel of John. It is time now for a chapter on the first Letter of John, which was probably composed after the gospel. In fact, it describes a situation that did not exist at the time of the writing of the gospel: a serious division within the Johannine Church.

Some Christians had separated themselves from the community and were very hostile to it. Were they docetists or spirituals with gnostic leanings or even gnostics in the full sense? The question is debated, but this is not the place for drawing a composite picture of these adversaries.[1]

The author of the letter addresses the Christians of the community and, following the logic of the Johannine tradition, describes the authentic face of a Christian community

---

1. See the commentaries for a detailed description of the scholarly hypotheses; see especially R. E. Brown, *The Epistles of John* (Anchor Bible 30; Garden City, NY: Doubleday, 1982) and R. Schnackenburg, *Die Johannesbriefe* (Freiburg i. B.: Herder, 1970).

and its deepest identity and urges it to be faithful to its true self. At the same time, however, he never loses sight of the controversy with the dissidents.

Communion with God

I cannot here go into all the arguments the author offers in trying to enlighten and convince his readers. I shall dwell rather on the question that closely concerns us, which is also the important question in the letter: communion with God.

As a matter of fact, the dissidents, too, declared: "We are in communion with him" (1:6). Everything suggests that they claimed to "dwell in God," to "know God," to "walk in the light," that is, to live in a higher spiritual dimension, in the name of which they assigned no importance to the commitments of everyday life.[2] John sharply rejects the idea of a relationship with God that is unmediated and completely interior; he rejects "the claim to a *direct* relationship with God that intends to bypass the brethren and the witnesses to the tradition (1 Jn 1:1-3; 4:6), that is, the Christian community (2:9-11; 3:11-18; 4:7-8, 11-12, 16, 19-21; 5:1-3). The reason for the rejection: The commandment of God includes, inseparably, both faith in Jesus and love for the brethren (3:23)."[3]

In John's view, only a community that bases itself on the original preaching of eyewitnesses of Jesus Christ, and therefore on authentic tradition, can mediate salvation.

2. See A. Dalbesio, *Quello che abbiamo udito e veduto* (Bologna: Edizioni Delhoniane, 1990) 93f.

3. Ibid., 96.

This is what John asserts from the Prologue of the letter onward. God has chosen a way of revealing himself which we may not ignore: The initiative comes from the Father; he has made himself known in his incarnate Son, who alone has seen and heard the Father (Jn 1:18; 3:11; 6:46; 12:50). Jesus made himself known to the Twelve, to men who had been able to see, hear, and touch him, and who became witnesses to him and were sent by him into the world; in order that they might carry out this task, they received the Paraclete, who, as they bear witness to Jesus, gives his own interior testimony to him.

> The consequence of this is clear: Mediating between the Father and the community of believers is the presence of the Son-Revealer, the Spirit of Christ, and eyewitnesses through whom the Spirit alone speaks. . . . It is therefore necessary to be in communion with the group of qualified witnesses in order to hear the authentic voice of the Spirit and so to enter into communion with Christ and through him with the Father.[4]

There is, then, no authentic communion with God if one ignores the historical Christ, and there is no real contact with Jesus if the tradition begun by his qualified witnesses is not accepted. In other words, "we must go by way of the ecclesial communion in order to reach communion with the divine persons."[5]

This is the meaning of the following statement: "What

---

4. Ibid., 123.
5. Ibid., 124.

we have seen and heard we proclaim also to you, so that you too may be in communion with us; and our communion is with the Father and with the Son, Jesus Christ" (1 Jn 1:3). But John does not limit himself to this statement; rather, in verse 7, he immediately expands the concept of *koinônia*: "This [communion] is no longer only a relationship between the You of the faithful, the We of the preachers, and God; it is a mutual relationship among all the members of the community."[6] If human beings are to have communion with God, they must not only be in communion with the witnesses and therefore with ecclesial tradition; they must also live lives of fraternal love. The two things are inseparable, because the substance of the tradition is precisely a summons to mutual love; it is the commandment that is simultaneously old and new. It is not surprising, then, that "this ecclesial communion, in the form of a fraternal life, is one of the dominant themes of 1 John, because it is an essential part of the author's message, which aims at checking doctrinal errors of the individualistic and self-centered kind held by the deviationists."[7]

---

6. Ibid., 131. Logic would make us expect to read in 1 John 1:7: "We are in communion with him [= God]." But, in opposition to the dissidents, who thought they could have an individualistic experience of God, the author says that the road to the light and therefore the truth is sure only if travelled in fraternal love; he "knows, as a way to God, only the way that passes through the community, which is the guardian of Christ's message" (Schnackenburg, *Die Johannesbriefe*, commenting on 1 John 1:7).

In the Old Testament writings, the expression "to walk in the light" means to lead a life in conformity with the law of God (Dt 16:4; Lv 26:3; Ps 89:16; 101:6; etc.). "In John, the expression connotes, in an increasingly profound degree, the sphere in which the human life of the individual unfolds and which conditions his resultant moral actions" (Dalbesio, *Quello che abbiamo*, 131).

7. Dalbesio, ibid.

1. 1 John 2:3-11

1 John 2:3-11 is the first section devoted to love and placed in a broader perspective that studies the relationship between knowledge and action.

The section begins with a sentence that serves as a kind of title and gives utterance to the basic principle that marks authentic Christian life, in contrast to the persuasions of the adversaries:

> By this we know that we have known him:
> if we keep his commandments.
> (1 Jn 2:3)

The author here broaches the subject of "knowledge of God," which in its substance is synonymous with "communion with God"; each of the two bear the impress of the same reality: mutual love.[8]

We must take note of how realistic John is. His interior certainty ("we know") of existing in the truth comes not from subjective impressions or feelings but from a very concrete fact: the fact of keeping God's commandments. In saying this, the author of the letter dismisses as inadequate and deceptive such other ways as ecstasy, speculation, or discussions about God. There is no authentic and life-giving knowledge of him without obedience to his will, that is, without letting one's life be determined by him and therefore without being vitally attuned to his life.

Those who claim to know God and do not manifest this

---

8. R. Bultmann, *The Johannine Letters* (Philadelphia: Fortress, 1973), commenting on 1 John 2.

knowledge in their actions show that they are liars. As P. Bonnard points out, they are not liars because they lie to deceive the brethren; they are liars because, even if they do not realize it, they are living a lie, living in a religious illusion. They are "sincere liars."[9]

In the positive statement in verse 5—"but those who keep his word, in them the love of God is truly perfect"—we see the characteristic shift from the plural to the singular: The observance of the commandments become the observance of his word.[10] The word means the commandments but summed up in a demand that is the heart of the commandments. For the moment, John remains focused on his own argument, that is, on the criterion of authentic communion with God. If believers are motivated by the love that comes from God,[11] they become "lovers" and show this love not by withdrawing into a purely interior relationship with God but by seeking the goal which God himself wants his love to have, namely, unity with the brethren. It is this concrete love for the brother or sister that is the sign that divine love dwells in the believers; if the love that comes from God is in us, there is no point in looking for a communion with God elsewhere, apart from the community.

Verse 6 makes this explicit by an appeal to the behavior of Jesus: "Anyone who says he dwells in Christ must behave as he behaved."

---

9. P. Bonnard, *Les épîtres johanniques* (Geneva: Labor et Fides, 1983), commenting on 1 John 2.

10. See also Jn 14:15, 25; 15:10; 2 Jn 4-6.

11. In "love of God" in verse 5, the genitive case can be understood as either objective or subjective. Exegetes generally prefer to take it as subjective: "the love that comes from God." An exception is Bonnard, *Les épîtres johanniques*, who thinks the words mean "our love for God."

Believers must therefore walk in obedience to the Father's will, an obedience that is crowned by the gift of their life for their fellows. What is meant is certainly not a purely external imitation, because this way of acting, which has its origin in the love of the Father who dwells in Christ and in believers, shows that there is true kinship between the two. Love of the brethren is part of life in God.[12]

In verses 7-8 John tells us in what this commandment, this word heard and therefore accepted, consists. It is the commandment that is both old and new:

Beloved, I am not writing you a new commandment,
but an old commandment,
which you received from the beginning.
The old commandment is the word
which you have heard.
And yet it *is* a new commandment
that I write to you:
It is true in him and in you,
because the darkness is dissipating
and the true light is already shining.

The commandment is certainly not new in the sense that the addressees of the letter are hearing it for the first time; by that standard, the commandment is old, since the teaching of the commandment of mutual love is a fundamental element of the Johannine catechesis that was given to the baptized.[13] In addition, it is certainly not a teaching

12. See ibid.
13. See J. Blank, *Studien zur biblischen Theologie* (SBANT 13; Stuttgart, 1992) 173

peculiar to the Johannine Church; Paul gives the same teaching in his very first letter.[14]

There is no doubt about the fact that in the early Church conversion and acceptance of the faith took the concrete form of incorporation into a life of fraternal love; it was this that made the commandment "new."[15] The newness did not, however, consist in mutual love understood as a social mark of a community; that phenomenon, that is, the demand for mutual love, was to be found in other communities as well.[16] The conviction that is displayed in John's letter is rather this: Fraternal love lived out in the community after the model of Jesus is the sign that God has shown his love for the human race in a definitive way. He has communicated the law governing his own life to believers, who through their fraternal love are received into the vital communion among the divine persons.

In this sense, mutual love is a new beginning; it is the sign that human beings have passed from darkness to light, from death to life, or, in other words, that they are already experiencing a new, eschatological reality even while still living in this world.

Everything has changed, because with the living of the new commandment light has appeared in the darkness and a new age has begun.[17]

---

14. 1 Thes 3:12; 4:9-10; see also 1 Pt 1:22f., which shows again that the commandment of mutual love was an integral part of instruction for baptism.

15. The author is probably referring to the gospel and to the verse: "I give you a new commandment" (Jn 13:34).

16. We may think, for example, of Qumran: *CD* 6, 14. 20-21.

17. See F. Fleinert-Jensen, *Commentaire de la Première Epître de Jean* (Lire la Bible 56; Paris: Cerf, 1982), comment on verse 8.

2. 1 John 3:11-23

1 John 3:11-23 marks the beginning of a new development of the idea of *agapê*, according to which the life of fraternal love is related to the love of Christ. The passage as a whole, however, does not seem to be highly unified and appears to have been composed of bits of catechesis that are applied here to the debate with the dissidents who are implicitly being addressed in the letter.[18]

John again harks back to the instruction given in the baptismal catechesis (v. 11): Love marks the entire existence of Christians. The statement seems almost to be a title: "This is the message you have heard from the beginning: that we are to love one another" (v. 11).

The author continues in a surprising way with a strong contrast, by offering Cain as an example of love's opposite: The hatred that leads to murder belongs in the realm of death, the sphere that "is not of God."

In contrast, where love is strong, life reigns, the life of God that leads to behavior opposite to that of Cain. It leads those who love to give life to a brother or sister instead of taking it away.

18. See especially the commentaries of Bonnard, *Les épîtres johanniques* and Schnackenburg, *Die Johannesbriefe*. Some details: the example of Cain in verse 12 is unexpected; verse 13 seems out of context; verses 19-22 are difficult to interpret. Perhaps, in an implicit attack on the adversaries, who were trying to tranquillize their consciences regarding a direct and wholly interior relationship with God, the author is emphasizing the objective and realistic criterion of observance of the commandments and thus of fraternal love. But this very orientation takes away the psychological security which an individualistic quest of God can give, either because the former leads believers not to think of themselves or because when it comes to love, one always falls short of its demands. The author shares his own serenity by telling his readers that a life of unity is an objective norm of tranquillity and a source of trust in God.

It could not be otherwise. Those who live lives of fraternal love show that they are from God, and whoever is from God cannot fail to love one's brother or sister. This is a vital demand that flows from the very being of the Christian.[19]

In verse 14 we read: "We know that we have passed from death to life, because we love the brothers and sisters."[20] Love of others is a sign of communion with God, who is Life. Spicq sums up: "Love is thus made the focal point of the entire Christian economy. In the Church (for it is still a question of loving the brothers and sisters) to live is to love."[21]

Verse 16 makes clear the nature and measure of *agapê*:

By this we have known love:
He has given his life for us;
therefore we too should give our life for the brethren.

In creation and history, and especially in the history of Israel, God had already shown the face of love, which, moreover, already existed among human beings. But now, in the Son, who was sent to save the human race, divine love has taken on the character of a definitive revelation that reached its full manifestation in the gift of the Son's

---

19. N. Lazure, *Les Valeurs morales de la Théologie johannique* (Paris: Gabalda, 1965) 247.

20. Bonnard points out the difference between this verse and John 5:24, which says: "Whoever hears my word and believes in the one who sent me has passed from death to life." The criterion for passing from death to life in 1 John 3:11 is no longer faith, as in the gospel, but fraternal love. The exegete inquires: Is John here perhaps resisting a conception of this "passage" in which fraternal love played no part? (*Les épîtres johanniques*, 77, note 1).

21. C. Spicq, *Apapè dans le Nouveau Testament* 3 (Paris: Gabalda, 1959) 258.

life on the cross. Love "reaches its height at the moment when it is annihilated."[22]

In the crucified Jesus love acquires its definitive, personalized features, and, in consequence, the demand created by that love also becomes clear. The source and standard of this demand are not to be found in a categorical imperative but in the historical destiny of Jesus of Nazareth.[23]

Verse 17 gives a concrete example to bring out what "giving one's life" means in the everyday life of believers. What is demanded is an unreserved love[24] in relations with others, and this kind of love cannot fail to show itself in concrete actions.

If someone possesses this world's riches,
but, seeing his brother in need,
closes his "entrails" against him,
how does the love of God dwell in him?

The theme was probably classical (see Jas 2:15f.), but the choice of words is revealing. Is it possible to read into this statement, by contrast, one element in the portrait of the dissidents? They would be rich but egocentric individuals, who preach fine sermons but do not go on to actions. John's language here is especially realistic, when he speaks of the "entrails" of a person who is moved to compassion in his innermost depths,[25] and when he uses a verb (*kleiô*) that means "to shut and bar a door."[26]

---

22. Fleinert-Jensen, *Commentaire* (note 17, above), on 1 Jn 3:11-23.
23. Bonnard, *Les épîtres johanniques*, on 1 Jn 3.
24. Ibid.
25. For an application to God see Lk 1:78: "through the entrails of the mercy of our God," that is, from the innermost depths of his love for humanity.
26. Spicq, *Agapè*, 3:261.

Anyone who refuses concrete help to a brother or sister in need shows that "the love of God does not dwell in him." This statement can have several meanings which are not mutually exclusive:[27]

• How can anyone who does not love his brother or sister in concrete ways claim to love God (objective genitive)?

• Anyone who does not love his brother or sister makes it clear that the divine *agapê* (subjective genitive) does not dwell in him.

• Anyone who does not help the needy makes it clear that he does not possess the characteristic traits of the love revealed by God (genitive of quality), that is, the need to "give his life."

John therefore urges his readers to concrete action:

Little children, let us love
not with words or the tongue
but with deeds and in truth. (V. 18)[28]

In the author's eyes, what makes love authentic is not fine words about love nor feelings nor good intentions, but concrete actions done for the sake of the brethren, in keeping with the kind of love lived by Jesus ("in truth").

But the very obviousness of love shown to a brother or sister makes clear this love's transcendent source, which is not to be confused with philanthrophy. That source is the divine *agapê*, which achieves its goal in a life of unity. Fraternal love is necessarily a love anchored in faith and carried deep into the human heart by the Holy Spirit. It is

27. The genitive "of God" may be objective, subjective, or a genitive of quality.
28. See the same exhortation in Jas 1:22; 2:15ff.

therefore not by chance that in the conclusion of this section John mentions faith and the Holy Spirit for the first time:

> This is his commandment,
> that we believe in the Name of his Son, Jesus Christ,
> and that we love one another,
> according to the precept he gave us.
> Whoever keeps his commandments abides in God
> and he in him.
> And by this we know that he abides in us:
> by the Spirit he has given us. (Vv. 23-24)

Verse 23 sums up the essence of the human being's response to the final revelation of God, which has for its purpose to bring humanity into the bosom of the Father. This essence is faith in the person of Jesus, who is recognized and accepted in his reality as the Son who is from eternity turned toward the Father. But, because of the divine *agapê* received in the heart of the believer, this is faith that tends toward a life of unity with one's brothers and sisters and seeks to make a reality the fraternal communion that is the ultimate desire of God for humanity, namely, that they live in God after the manner of God. God, who is *agapê*, includes us in the circuit of his love.

Faith thus implies a "conversion" in the full sense of this term; it implies a self-forgetfulness in love of God and the brethren.[29]

For this reason, "whoever keeps his commandments," in the Johannine sense of this phrase, that is, who directs his

---

29. See Lazure, *Les Valeurs morales*, 251.

entire life and behavior to the actuation of mutual love in the community, lives in perfect communion with God.[30]

Understanding of this truth is given by the Holy Spirit, who communicates the deeper, luminous meaning of a life lived in faith and mutual love, by showing it to be a life lived in the divine communion. Verse 24, then, refers to the Holy Spirit in his role as revealer.

3. *1 John 4:7–5:2*

John returns once again to the subject of love, using words that are more incisive and radical than ever. The subject is obviously one especially close to his heart.

This section can be subdivided into several short literary units.

In the first (vv. 7-10), which is introduced by the epithet "beloved," the author stresses the nature and origin of *agapê*:

Beloved (*agapêtoi*), let us love (*agapômen*) one another,
for love (*agapê*) is from God,
and whoever loves (*ho agapôn*) is begotten by God
and knows God.
Whoever does not love has not known God,
for God is love.

---

30. In order to bring out the closeness and completeness of the relationship between God and believers, the author uses the formula of mutual immanence—"he abides in God and God in him"—which is repeated three times in the next section (1 Jn 4:13, 15, 16). This is something the evangelist avoids in principle, since he is emphasizing the mediation of Christ. The author of the letter, however, takes the mediation for granted and uses the formula of mutual immanence to describe the complete and definitive indwelling of God in human beings and vice versa.

The love of God has shown itself among us in this:
God sent his only-begotten Son into the world,
in order that we might have life through him.
In this (is) love: not that we have loved God
but that he loved us and sent his Son
as expiation for our sins.

In 1 John 3:11 and 23, John had based his claim that there is no authentic love of God apart from love of the brethren on the fact that only those who obey the divine will truly love God. Here—still in opposition to those who thought they could love God while spiting their neighbor—John presents the *necessity* of fraternal love not only as a response to the commandment of God but also as a natural necessity, since love comes from God and has its roots in God.[31] As C. Spicq says, love is not "mere fidelity to a commandment but is a demand of nature"[32] for those who believe in Jesus. The divine *agapê* is communicated as a gift that "informs" human love and impels the believer to love others in concrete ways. More than that: The divine *agapê* that is given to us is the hidden spring that takes hold of the entire person and places it in a state of love, thus defining the believer as "one who loves" (*ho agapôn*), "a being who constantly has the active attitude of a lover."[33]

Since love of one's brethren is grounded in the love of God, it is no longer simply an act of submission to a commandment imposed from without but becomes an

31. "Love is from (= belongs to) God": a typically Johannine expression. The author is showing the sphere to which a given reality *belongs* by pointing to its *origin*. See Dalbesio, *Quello che abbiamo*, 184.
32. Spicq, *Agapè* 3:270.
33. Dalbesio, *Quello che abbiamo*, 185.

action in keeping with the nature of the "new self," the most personal action of the believer as child of God.

God created human beings in his own image and likeness, but now this likeness has moved to a new level. It no longer comes only through the act of creation but through faith and love;[34] it is no longer an external likeness but a form of "consubstantiality."

It is then possible to go back from effects to cause. Fraternal love is the criterion of an authentic relationship with God; it shows that the person who loves has been begotten by God and has true knowledge of him, that is, the kind of knowledge that presupposes a vital communion with him.

In verse 8 John says as much in negative form: Those who do not love the brethren show that they are shut in on themselves, and this condition logically means that they are also closed against the divine *agapê*.

The author has no doubt. The claim to love God without loving one's brethren contains an intrinsic contradiction. Effect cannot be separated from cause; mutual love cannot be separated from its source, the divine *agapê*.

Indeed, "God is love," John writes a first time.[35]

This is not a philosophical definition of the divine Being. It is something the author of the letter infers as he considers God's action in history. At the same time, however, "the description is not purely functional . . . for if God is love toward us, it is because he is love in himself."[36]

In the present context, John's statement is in the service

34. See Brown, *The Epistles of John*, 548.
35. See also 1 Jn 4:16.
36. Brown, *The Epistles of John*, 549.

of the argument that only love can know love. For this reason, an authentic love of God necessarily arises by way of fraternal love. It is obvious that in John's thinking knowledge of God is not a matter of merely listing some divine attributes. It means rather to have "an intense experience of what God is in himself."[37] This requires a vital communion with him that cannot exist apart from a real love.

In verses 9-10 John explains further the statement, "God is love," of verse 8. This is not an abstract definition, nor is it the result of reflection on the qualities of God, as these may be inferred from human qualities or from human dreams that are projected onto God.

To the eyes of believers, God himself has made his love visible in a definitive way through a particular historical event: the Jesus-event, the only-begotten Son, the humanized expression of divine love.

In thus sending and giving his own Son, God gives everything he has; he gives his entire self, and therefore reveals not simply this or that divine attribute but his innermost identity.

Twice in succession (vv. 9-10) John writes that God has *sent* his Son, thereby using traditional expressions which he does not think it necessary to explain. The first time he uses this language in order to say that the divine love historically manifested in the sending of the Son has a purpose: to give life to human beings by making them sharers in the very life of God. The second time it is to show that in carrying out its plan, this love had to overcome the alienation of humanity from God, that is, sin.

---

37. Dalbesio, *Quello che abbiamo*, 189.

Now, as the author says in verse 10, it is characteristic of divine love that it is *first*. John knows, of course, that since human beings are created in the image of God, they have always had hearts capable of loving. However, the sacred writer is not thinking of the various qualities or degrees of human love but of the love known as *agapê*, which is possible only because God has taken the initiative. Therefore Christian love, with all that makes it new, can only be a response to God's love, which is first.

> These verses show Christianity to be a religion of love, not [only], however, in the sense that love is the center of Christian teaching, but, much more importantly, because human beings know what love really is only from the sending of the Son of God and since the time when they experienced this fullness of love, this divine love, within themselves.[38]

Verses 11-13 form a second unit:

> Beloved, if God has so loved us,
> then we ought to love one another.
> No one has ever seen God:
> If we love one another,
> God remains in us
> and his love in us is perfect.
> By this we know that we remain in him and he in us,
> that he has given us his Spirit.

Previously the author has been bringing out the characteristics of God's love as the source of Christian love. Now,

---

38. Schnackenburg, *Die Johannesbriefe*, commenting on 1 Jn 4:7–5:2.

with the clause, "if God has so loved us," he turns his attention to the way of loving God. Divine love becomes the model of our love and, at the same time, motivates the duty of loving.

The argument in verse 11 is an unexpected one: Given the conditional clause, "if God has so loved us," we would naturally expect as the conclusion, "then we should love God." Instead, John concludes: "then we ought to love one another." This is a sign, once again, of the author's concern not to separate love of God from concrete love of the brethren.

Mutual love should also imitate God's way of loving as shown in the sending of the Son. It should, that is, be a love that breaks out of a closed circle and turns to others: an outgoing love,[39] marked by utterly free giving.

In verse 12, John repeats a biblical certainty already expressed at the beginning of the gospel (1:18): For human beings in their earthly state a direct vision of God is impossible. Communion with God, however, is possible even now, and it is achieved not by a contemplative effort but by mutual love. God, the God of revelation, is not reached, therefore, by means of ascetical and ecstatic techniques; rather, it is God who comes to us and dwells within us when we love one another.

But, faithful as he is to the idea of revelation, John does not attribute the initiative here to human beings. It is not the love of believers that merits and elicits the divine presence. Rather, mutual love is the proof that God is present and acting; it is the proof that the *agapê* of God is

---

39. Brown, *The Epistles of John*, 554.

at the source of our love and therefore of our communion with the invisible One.

John adds: "And his love in us is perfect." He probably[40] means that the *agapê* that comes from God achieves its purpose in our mutual love.[41]

F. Fleinert-Jensen carries the thought further: "Wherever love creates a communion among human beings, what takes place is not simply a human encounter but also an encounter with the love of God that finds its fulfillment *in us*. . . . Wherever love becomes a reality, it can be interpreted as not only made possible by God but also used by him as an event through which he acts and expresses himself."[42] Through the reality of love God "insinuates himself" into history and accomplishes his will, even if human beings do not realize this.

The fact that mutual love brings about an intimacy with God is attested by the Holy Spirit, as verse 13 says.

Verses 14-16 and 17-18 (although these last two are not

---

40. "And (*kai*) his (*autou*) love in us (*en hêmin*) is perfect." The statement can be interpreted in several ways.

The "and" (*kai*) can

a) be consecutive: the fact that God dwells in us has for a consequence that his love in us is perfect;

b) adjunctive: in mutual love God dwells in us, and, in addition, his love in us is perfect;

c) explanatory: God dwells in us, that is to say, his love in us is perfect. The possessive "his" (*autou*) can be:

a) a subjective genitive: the love that comes from God is perfect in us.

b) an objective genitive: love for God is perfect, that is, authentic, when we live in mutual love.

c) Schnackenburg suggests a genitive of quality: the love *characteristic* of God.

41. "In us" (*en hêmin*) points to the presence of God in the community (= "among us") rather than within each person, although this last is not excluded.

42. Fleinert-Jensen, *Commentaire*, on 1 Jn 4:11-13.

directly related to the subject we are dealing with) seem to be a complement that momentarily interrupts the course of thought, which is immediately picked up again in verse 19.

And we have seen and we bear witness
that the Father sent his Son as Savior of the world.
Whoever confess that Jesus is the Son of God,
in them God abides
and they in God.
And we have known and have believed
in the love God has for us.
God is love, and those who abide in love
abide in God and God abides in them. (Vv. 14-16)

While God cannot be seen in himself, it is possible to see, through faith, the love of the Father as manifested historically in the sending of the Savior. It is by reason of this vision that the author is able, as he did earlier in the Prologue of the letter, to appeal to his own experience as an eyewitness, along with the other disciples of the early days.

John harks back here to the theme of faith: Belief in Christ consists in an unreserved acceptance of his person, because one has recognized in the man Jesus of Nazareth the divine face of the Son, which in turn manifests the Father's love for us (see v. 9).

It is this acceptance that brings believers into communion with God and therefore into lifegiving contact with the divine *agapê*, which in turn is the permanent source of openness to and unconditional love for the brethren. As a result, this love for the brethren becomes a sign of communion with God.

John sums up his thought in verse 16, which is

> a high point in Johannine contemplation and perhaps
> the most complete expression of the Johannine mes-
> sage, of the demand made upon and the promises made
> to humanity. [The verse] proclaims the Christian God
> who has revealed his love in Christ; the latter calls
> believers to an attitude of love and to action in accord
> with the loftiest model, and promises them a perma-
> nent communion with this God of love, in whom the
> love of believers likewise has its source and from which
> it derives its power and receives its reward.[43]

John picks up the thread of his thought (left off in v. 13)
on the necessity of loving one's brethren if we are to live in
an authentic relationship with God. The ideas are not new,
but the controversy with those who were claiming to love
God without loving their neighbor compels the writer to
insist on the point and to show the indispensable connection between love of God and love of other human beings:

> We must love because he has first loved us.
> If someone says: "I love God,"
> and then hates his own brother,
> he is a liar.
> One who does not love the brother whom he sees
> cannot love God whom he does not see.
> And we have [received] this commandment
>   from him:
> whoever loves God also loves his brother. (Vv. 19-21)

---

43. Schnackenburg, *Die Johannesbriefe*, on 1 Jn 4:16.

The first argument (v. 19) can be variously interpreted.[44] If the verb "we love" is read as in the indicative mood, the verse seems to be a reply of John to the adversaries: Our love is not our own creation but has its origin in God and—this is implied—is therefore authentic.

It is preferable to read the verb as an imperative. In this case, the verse can have two meanings:

• Since God is the source of *agapê* in us, love becomes an obligation in keeping with the new being of the believers;

• The experience of encounter with God who forgives renews the person and impels him or her to love others in turn, in keeping with, for example, the teaching in the parable of the merciless servant (Mt 18:23ff.).

In any case, our love is always a response to the *agapê* which God has bestowed on us.

Verse 20 seems to refer to some action of the dissidents and recalls 1 John 2:4. It offers a new occasion for asserting the close connection between love of God and love of one's brothers and sisters. The author insists that there is no authentic love for God without love for one's neighbor; since the one does not exist without the other, the one can serve as a criterion for determining the truth of the other.[45] Those who claim the contrary are not living in the truth but are completely deluding themselves. John proves this with an argument that seems to proceed from the lesser to the greater (*a minori ad maius*): Those unable to love the brothers and sisters whom they see will be unable to love God whom

---

44. *Hêmeis agapômen* (translated here as "we must love")) can be indicative or imperative. Moreover, the object of the verb "love" is in doubt: God? the brethren? or is the author simply speaking of love as such?

45. Beyond any doubt, John does not mean to say that love for God is identical with and coextensive with love of the brethren.

they do not see. Put in this way, the argument is uncon-
vincing, since, as the dissident Christians show, it is easier
to claim to love God than to love the brethren in concrete
ways! It is better, then, to understand verse 20 in this way:
Only those who love their brothers and sisters in concrete
ways prove that they truly love God.[46]

Verse 21 offers a further argument to show that the
adversaries are deluding themselves: They forget that God
has, through Jesus, given a commandment, that of mutual
love (1 Jn 2:7f.; 3:23; see Jn 13:34f.). Every Jew and every
Christian knows that love of God is attested by observance
of the commandments (theology of the covenant).[47] Consequently, it is only through obedience to the divine will,
which is summed up in the commandment of fraternal love,
that we prove we love God.[48]

John's emphasis on love of one's brothers and sisters, and
not of one's neighbor in general, demands that we not forget
the viewpoint of the author and the situation in which the
letter was written (a situation resulting from a crisis within
the Church itself). John's point of reference is Christians
who have distanced themselves from the community by

---

46. See Bonnard, *Les épîtres joahnniques*, commenting on 1 Jn 4:19-21.

47. St. Augustine, *Homilies on the First Letter of John*: "How can you love the
God whose commandment you hate? Who would ever say: 'I love the
emperor, but I hate his laws'? . . . What is the law of our sovereign? 'I give
you a new commandment: that you love one another.' You say you love
Christ: observe his commandment and love your brother. If you do not
love your brother, how can you love one whose commandment you
despise?"

48. Verse 21 recalls, as simply an external fact, the twofold commandment
given by Jesus: to love God and love one's neighbor. The problem and
arguments of the first Letter of John are different: The author is proving
that there is no authentic love of God apart from mutual love in the
community.

breaking their links to other Christians and claiming to possess the true knowledge of God.

As a result of this situation, John focuses his attention on love of the brethren and therefore on mutuality, on the love that brings about unity. The breaking of unity is a clear sign of the "lie" in which the dissidents are living.

The final unit that interests us here—1 John 5:12—concludes the section on *agapê* that began in 1 John 4:7.[49]

> Whoever believes that Jesus the Christ is born of God
> and whoever loves the begetter
> loves also the one begotten by him.
> By this we know that we love the children of God,
> if[50] we love God and carry out his commandments.

John starts from the beginning, from the belief that Jesus is the Christ, that is, that the Christ is precisely Jesus of Nazareth (which the dissidents deny: 1 Jn 2:24; 4:2f.; 2 Jn 7), and he leads his readers to a logical conclusion that shows the dissidents once again to be wrong.

Those who believe show thereby that they are born of God; those born of God love. But verse 1 adds a further argument that starts with a point regarded as obvious: Believers obviously love God who through faith has begotten them for a life as his children; in other words, they love God as truly a father to them. John thus starts from the Father-children relationship that exists between God and believers, and he concludes that Christians will logically love the other children of God, who are their brothers and

---

49. Note the inclusion created by "born of God" in 4:7 and 5:1-2.
50. *Hotan* ("whenever") here is probably equivalent to *ean* ("if").

sisters. From this it follows that the dissidents' lack of love for other believers has something unnatural about it.[51]

The logic of verse 2, on the other hand, is surprising. The author turns around the argument he has been using thus far (4:7f., 20f.; 5:1), namely, that fraternal love truly lived is a sign of an authentic relationship with God. Now he says that love of God leads to an authentic love of the brethren. Is love of God the criterion of love of the brethren? A condition for it? Is love of God as shown in the observance of his commandments also a sign of an authentic love of the brethren or is it necessary in order to be able truly to love the brethren? In relation to verse 1, the second alternative is preferable, that is, only a love rooted in God and coming from faith is an authentic love of others as "brothers and sisters" because they are children of God.

The fact that John inverts the terms of the argument simply confirms the close unity which he sees between love of God and love of one's brethren.

As we read through the first Letter of John, we are struck by the predominance of the theme of love and in particular of fraternal love, that is, a love lived as an expression of the unity of the community.

John warns of various dangers: of limiting love to "fine words" without ever moving on to actions; of thinking about God as Love in an abstract way, apart from his historical manifestation in Jesus; the danger, above all, of succumbing to the illusory claim to love God while breaking away from the unity of the community. On the contrary, communion with God demands communion with one's

---

51. See Schnackenburg, *Die Johannesbriefe*, on 1 Jn 5.

brothers and sisters, for this alone is the criterion of an authentic love of God.

This letter of John, when looked at in all its parts, appears with increasing clarity to be not a calm, atemporal instruction on love of God and neighbor, but as a polemical writing addressed to a concrete community that is passing through a serious internal crisis. Such a situation only brings out more clearly the importance and extreme relevance of the author's statements and his strong consciousness of the fact that mutual love, the love that brings unity, is the divine characteristic of the Church. This love is that which from the outset has constituted and now constitutes the Church's true identity, which must be preserved at any cost.

Fraternal love is by its nature the sign par excellence of a true communion with God. Wherever this love is a reality, the *agapê* of God has reached its goal: "that all may be one as we are one."

Conclusion

The result of our journey through the writings of John is the undeniable conclusion that it is impossible to read a spirituality of an individualistic kind into his theology and ethics. The rhetorical question of J. M. R. Tillard which I cited in my Preface—whether the life of communion among believers should be regarded as simply a means to reach an alone-with-the-Alone relationship with the eternal God—has likewise been given a definitely negative answer.

As a matter of fact, in John's perspective everything promotes a spirituality of communion. God's plan for humanity was begun in the crucified and risen Jesus, who brings together into unity, that is, into himself, the scattered children of God (Jn 11:52), in order that they may live the life of oneness of the divine persons. There is no goal apart from this plan; there is no place for an everlasting private devotion. Instead, it is in unity that each person grows toward a personal completion, thanks to others and in permanent communion with others, and will experience an entirely personal filial relationship with the Father and with Jesus, the Son.

But this new humanity is not something solely of the future. As is true of every reality of faith, in Jesus God has given us everything; it is up to us to accept it and put it into practice in the present time.

> The glory that you have given to me,
> I have given to them,
> so that, like us, they may be a single thing.
> (Jn 17:22)

The Italian Ecumenical Translation of the Bible has an excellent comment on this passage:

The glory which Christ obtains from the Father beyond the cross (17:1-5) is the manifestation to humanity of his indescribable communion with the Father. Believers who grasp this are themselves associated with it and become in their turn a manifestation of the glory of Christ. This takes place concretely in the unity which they bring about by loving one another.

In John's view, the whole of Christian ethics flows from the actualization of the unity described in the prayer in John 17. From this unity comes the importance assigned to faith and to love in its full form as mutual love. The opening of the human mind and heart to the proclamation of the gospel is fundamental, because it enables the person to see in Jesus the one sent by God. This Jesus is the mirror of God's unalterable love for humanity; he is the revelation of the Son who is from eternity turned toward the bosom of the Father, but also has a human love that he experienced on earth and that is a manifestation of the divine intimacy henceforth available to humanity. The life of the Trinity is set before believers as the place and model of the relationship that is to exist among them. Therefore, with complete consistency, John focuses his attention on mutual love, which is a love anchored in the divine *agapê*.

The evangelist does not distance himself from the structure of the covenant. Now, however, the observance of the commandments is no longer directed to a scrupulous practice of countless precepts but to the many demands of a life of unity. It is in a life of communion with one's brothers and sisters that believers live out the full communion with God that he has offered to them in Jesus.

This communion necessarily supposes a Christological dimension: In order to live a filial relationship with the Father within the Trinity, Christians receive the relationship of the Son with the Father. A deep and mysterious relationship of identity thus arises between believers and Jesus; the evangelist expresses this relationship in the formula of mutual immanence or indwelling, especially in connection with the eucharist (Jn 6:56).

When believers, as children of God, are placed in the bosom of the Father, they experience the Father's love and find an I–thou relationship with Jesus (Jn 14:21; 17:26; 1 Jn 1:3).

There is no need to repeat once again that although this last relationship is eminently personal, it is not a private event. Being "in Christ" brings human beings close to one another. It is through "being *one*" that they share in the life of unity of the divine persons.

The spirituality of communion, which is given its theological statement in the gospel, emerges powerfully in the first Letter of John, in the course of a controversy with Christians who claimed to have a relationship with God but did not also love their brothers and sisters and even separated themselves from the community.

The author uses various arguments in an effort to persuade his readers of the inconsistency of such a position. To this end he constantly brings out the close connection between the horizontal dimension of love (love of one's brothers and sisters) and its vertical dimension (love of God). As a result, fraternal love in all its concreteness becomes the criterion of the authenticity of love of God.

The author, I repeat, uses various arguments. Thus he appeals, in a way understandable by every Christian who knows the Bible, to the obvious truth that love for God is manifested not in feelings or fine words but in obedience to his commandments, which now focus chiefly on fraternal love.

But John delves more deeply: Love for the brethren is not simply observance of a commandment but a demand of nature. Because believers are born of God they participate in the divine *agapê* and are thereby turned essentially into "lovers." Here, if anywhere, the saying, "Like father, like son," applies. The children of God will "spontaneously" imitate their Father, not by turning inward for a relationship of exclusive intimacy, but by giving their own love the outgoing and unitive characteristics of the divine love, the measure of which, following the example of Jesus, is the gift of one's life.

Furthermore, having become children of God, believers undoubtedly direct their filial love essentially to the Father, but, on the other hand and in consequence, they cannot fail to love all those whom the Father has begotten as his children and who are therefore their brothers and sisters.

Love for human beings, which reaches its natural full form in fraternal love within the community, is the unmistakable sign that we have passed from death to life.

I end with a few words of Augustine: "If you love the brother whom you see, you will at the same time be able to see God, because you will see love itself, and God dwells in love."[1]

---

1. Augustine, *Homilies on the First Letter of John*. Note this passage, too: "Why does this man not see God? Because he does not have love itself. He does not see God precisely because he does not have love. And he does not have love because he does not love his brother. Therefore he does not see God because he does not have love" (ibid.).

Bibliography

Blank, J. *Das Evangelium nach Johannes*. 4 vols. Düsseldorf: Patmos, 1981.

Bonnard, P. *Les épîtres johanniques*. Geneva: Labor et Fides, 1983.

Bonsirven, J. *Epîtres de Saint Jean*. Verbum Salutis 9. Paris: Beauchesne, 1954.

Braun, F. M. *La foi chrétienne selon Saint Jean*. Paris: Gabalda, 1976.

_____. *Jean le Théologien*. 4 vols. Paris: Gabalda, 1959.

Brown, R. E. *The Gospel according to John*. 2 vols.; Anchor Bible 29 and 29A. Garden City, NY: Doubleday, 1966 and 1970.

_____. *The Epistles of John*. Anchor Bible 30. Garden City, NY: Doubleday, 1982.

Bultmann, R. *The Johannine Letters*. Philadelphia: Fortress, 1973.

Cilia, L. *La morte di Gesù e l'unità degli uomini (Gv 11, 47-53; 12, 32)*. Bologna: Edizioni Delhoniane, 1992. Supplement to *Rivista Biblica*, vol. 24.

Dalbesio, A. *Quello che abbiamo udito e veduto*. Bologna: Edizioni Delhoniane, 1990. Supplement to *Rivista Biblica*, vol. 22.

de la Potterie, I. *Gesù Verità*. Turin: Marietti, 1973.

_____. *La Vérité dans Saint Jean*. Rome: Biblical Institute Press, 1977.

_____. *Studi di Cristologia giovannea*. Genoa: Marietti, 1986.

Dodd, C. H. *The Interpretation of the Fourth Gospel*. Cambridge: Cambridge University Press, 1953.

Exegetisches Wörterbuch zum Neuen Testament.

Feuillet, A. *Le Prologue du quatrième Evangile*. Paris: Desclée de Brouwer, 1968.

Fleinert-Jensen, F. *Commentaire de la Première Epître de Jean*. Lire la

Bible 56. Paris: Cerf, 1982.

Huby, J. *Le Discours de Jésus après la Cène*. Paris: Beauchesne, 1942.

Lagrange, M. J. *L'Evangile selon Saint Jean*. Paris: Gabalda, 1936.

Lazure, N. *Les Valeurs morales de la Théologie johannique*. Paris: Gabalda, 1965.

Léon-Dufour, X. *Lettura del Vangelo secondo Giovanni*. 3 vols. Cinisello Balsamo-Milan, 1989, 1992, 1995.

Mannucci, U. *Giovanni, Vangelo narrante*. Bologna: Edizioni Delhoniane, 1993.

Onuki, T. *Gemeinde und Welt im Johannesevangelium*. WMANT 56. Neukirchen: Neukirchener Verlag, 1984.

Panimolle, S. A. *Lettura pastorale del Vangelo di Giovanni*. Bologna: Edizioni Dehoniane, 1978, 1984.

Rossé, G. *L'Ultima preghiera di Gesù — dal Vangelo di Giovanni*. Rome: Città Nuova, 1988.

Schlier, H. "Die Bruderliebe nach dem Evangelium und den Briefen des Johannes." *Mélanges Bibliques B. Rigaux*. Gembloux: Duculot, 1969. Pp. 235ff.

Schnackenburg, R. *The Gospel according to John*. Trans. K. Smyth, C. Hastings, D. Smith, and others. 3 vols. New York: Crossroad, 1982.

_____. *Die Johannesbriefe*. Freiburg: Herder, 1970[4].

_____. *Jesus in the Gospels: A Biblical Christology* St. Louisville, KY: The Westminister John Knox Press 1995.

_____. *Die sittliche Botschaft des Neuen Testaments*. 2 vols. Freiburg i. B.: Herder, 1988.

_____. *Le parole di commiato di Gesù (Gv 13–17)*. Brescia: Paideia, 1994.

Spicq, C. *Agapè dans le Nouveau Testament* 3. Paris: Gabalda, 1959.

Theological Dictionary of the New Testament (TDNT)

Vanni, U. *Il Vangelo secondo Giovanni. Passi scelti*. Rome: Pontifical Gregorian University, 1989.

Wikenhauser, A. *L'Evangelo secondo Giovanni*. Brescia: Morcelliana, 1966.

SPIRITUAL COMMENTARIES FROM NEW CITY PRESS

ROMANS
The Good News According to Paul
DANIEL HARRINGTON

"Here Daniel Harrington makes Paul a good spiritual director. This he achieves by coupling--but not mixing--delightfully straight exegesis with suggestive pointers toward Spiritual Exercises. He is an honest guide. He leads us to Paul's abiding insights. He also tells clearly when we know things that Paul did not." (Krister Stendahl, Harvard University)

ISBN 1-56548-096-1, paper, 5 3/8 x 8 1/2, 152 pp., $9.95

PAUL'S PRISON LETTERS
Scriptural Commentaries on Paul's Letters to Philemon, the Philippians, and the Colossians
DANIEL HARRINGTON

"I heartily recommend this work both for the person seeking an initial familiarity with Saint Paul, and for the more advanced student eager to link exegesis with classical Ignatian spirituality. This work enhances knowledge with imaginative meditation and prayer. Once again, Father Harrington's treatment and approach is superb." (Bishop Richard Sklba)

ISBN 1-56548-088-0, paper, 5 3/8 x 8 1/2, 144 pp., $9.95

MATTHEW
The First Gospel
RONALD D. WITHERUP

This "spiritual" commentary on the Gospel of Matthew offers a section-by-section reading by one of today's foremost experts. It employs the latest scholarship but leaves out technical language that is often difficult to follow and understand. Witherup offers his reflections for spiritual enrichment and practical application. Its perspective is ecumenical and its scope includes essential insights from literary, historical, and theological perspectives of the gospel.

ISBN 1-56548-123-2, paper, 5 3/8 x 8 1/2, 152 pp., $9.95

TO ORDER PHONE 1-800-462-5980

AND . . .

DANIEL
A book for Troubling Times
ALEXANDER A. DI LELLA

"The 'troubled times' of the title matches this century as well as the past—we are confronted by a timeless biblical work with a timely biblical commentary." (Roland E. Murphy, O. Carm.)

"Di Lella provides a wealth of interesting information, old and new, regarding the context and meaning of Daniel. In doing so he offers an interpretation for that ancient time and, more importantly, a pointed prophetic message for our time." (Rev. Arthur O. Van Eck, New Revised Standard Version Bible Project)

ISBN 1-56548-087-2, paper, 5 3/8 x 8 1/2, 160 pp., $11.95

SONG OF SONGS
The Love Poetry of Scripture
DIANNE BERGANT

Bergant's spiritual commentary is a delightfully intriguing literal reading of the Song of Songs. She develops and vividly explains the poetic elements of the sacred text and masterfully applies them to contemporary spirituality.

"Bergant combines the best of modern scholarship—contemporary interpretation theory, knowledge of the ancient Near East, and a close reading of the text—to draw forth insights which support contemporary spirituality. Her reading is sensitive to the integrity of creation and to the awesome and transforming power of human love. This is a rare biblical commentary—and like the Song itself, and the love of which the Song speaks, it is 'more delightful than wine.' " (*Alice L. Laffey*, College of the Holy Cross)

ISBN 1-56548-100-3, paper, 5 3/8 x 8 1/2, 152 pp., $9.95

TO ORDER PHONE 1-800-462-5980